Fossils for Kids

An Introduction to Paleontology

ACKNOWLEDGMENTS

Dan would like to thank his wife, Julie, for her unending support and love, and his parents, Bob and Nancy, for all their help. He'd also like to thank Steve Turnbull for his constant encouragement, and for being his fellow nature nerd for so many years.

Disclaimer This book is meant as an introduction to the world of fossils and paleontology. It does not guarantee your safety when fossil collecting in any way—when collecting, you do so at your own risk. Neither Adventure Publications nor Dan Lynch is liable for property loss or damage or personal injury that may result from fossil collecting. Before you go fossil collecting, be sure you have permission to collect on the location, ensure that an adult or adults are present, and always avoid potentially dangerous locations, such as cliffs, areas with moving/deep water, deserts, or areas where wildlife (bears, snakes, cacti, insects) may be a concern. Finally, be aware that many national, state, and local parks do not allow rock collecting, so again, only collect where you are allowed to do so.

Edited by Brett Ortler

All photos by Dan R. Lynch unless otherwise noted.
Jonathan Norberg: Hand (front cover); **ntv/Shutterstock.com:** Yellow Amber (front cover); **Brett Ortler:** 169 (both).

The Flickr images below are licensed under the Attribution-ShareAlike 2.0 Generic (CC BY-SA 2.0) license, which is available here: https://creativecommons.org/licenses/by-sa/2.0/
Dallas Krentzel: 110 (top left); **James St. John:** 57 (top), 69 (bottom); **Jim Naureckas:** 108; **Missbossy:** 59 (middle); **Travel Manitoba:** 62 (bottom).

The Flickr images below are licensed under the Public Domain Dedication (CCO 1.0) license, which is available here: https://creativecommons.org/publicdomain/
Gary Todd: 59 (top).

photo credits continue on page 188

10 9 8 7 6 5 4 3
Fossils for Kids: An Introduction to Palentology
Copyright © 2020 by Dan R. Lynch
Published by Adventure Publications, an imprint of AdventureKEEN
310 Garfield Street South, Cambridge, Minnesota 55008
(800) 678-7006
www.adventurepublications.net
All rights reserved
Printed in China
ISBN 978-1-59193-939-9 (pbk.); ISBN 978-1-59193-940-5 (ebook)

Fossils for Kids

An Introduction to Paleontology

Dan R. Lynch

Adventure Publications
Cambridge, Minnesota

Table of Contents

INTRODUCTION

All About Fossils 6

Types of Fossils 10

Fossils, Then and Now. 12

About Rocks 14

How Do Bones and Plants Get Inside Rocks? 22

Cells and Fossilization. 26

Other Ways Fossils Can Form 30

What Are Fossils Made Out Of? 33

Sedimentary Rocks that Can Have Fossils in Them . . 36

Ancient Life and Extinction 40

Rock Layers Tell a Story 42

TYPES OF FOSSILS

Animal Fossils

Dinosaurs 52

Reptiles 62

Amphibians. 65

Fish. 68

Sharks 72

Gastropods 75

Brachiopods and Bivalves. 78

Crustaceans. 81

Coral and Bryozoans 84

Crinoids and Blastoids. 87

Trilobites. 90

Ammonites, Baculites, Orthoceras,
Nautilus, and Belemnites. 93

Eurypterids 96

Sea Sponges, Algae, and Stromatolites 99

Echinoderms 102

Insects, Arachnids, and Myriapods 105

Mammals. 108

Plant Fossils and Amber

Ferns and Horsetails 114

Palms 117

Leaves, Stems, and Other Plant Fossils. 120

Ginkgo Trees. 124

Conifers and Pine Cones 127

Petrified Wood 130

Amber 133

Microfossils, Trace Fossils, Hydrocarbons, Coal, and Pseudofossils

Microfossils 138

Trace Fossils 141

Hydrocarbons 144

Coal 147

Pseudofossils 150

COLLECTING FOSSILS

Can I Collect Fossils Everywhere? 154

How Do I Stay Safe When Fossil Collecting? 156

Where to Look 158

How to Spot Fossils in Nature. 162

Signs of Fossils that You Should Look for 166

How Do You Collect Fossils? 168

How Scientists Collect Fossils 170

Identifying Fossils 171

Rock Shops and Buying Fossils 172

Replicas 174

Fake Fossils 174

COOL FOSSIL SITES AROUND THE U.S. 176

GLOSSARY 183

RECOMMENDED READING. 187

ABOUT THE AUTHOR 188

ALL ABOUT FOSSILS

The world is full of amazing plants and animals today, but before you or any other humans were born, Earth was once home to a wide variety of incredible plants and animals, including the mighty dinosaurs and the creepy-crawly trilobites. These animals lived millions of years ago—and then many died out. But we've never seen a living dinosaur, so how do we know what they looked like? The reason we know so much about ancient animals is because of their fossils.

Tyrannosaurus rex is one of the most famous dinosaurs—it had powerful legs and huge jaws.

Fossils are parts of dead plants and animals that have turned into minerals over a very long time. Some were left behind by animal varieties found today (such as sharks!), but many others are from types of animals that are **extinct** (long dead). We can find fossils all over the world by looking inside the right kinds of rocks. Common fossils include animal bones, teeth, and shells, as well as plant leaves and branches. By comparing fossils to living things, we can learn what ancient plants and animals looked like and learn about their lives, the environment they lived in, and even what they ate!

Finding fossils helps give us an idea what
ancient animals and plants might have looked
like, including *T. rex*.

But there are many other kinds of fossils! This
jaw is from an ancient short-necked giraffe.

Most fossils only show the hard parts of an animal, like this shell from an ammonite.

TYPES OF FOSSILS

There were lots of strange and amazing animals and plants that lived long ago. Some are no longer alive today, but some are still around! Here are just a few examples.

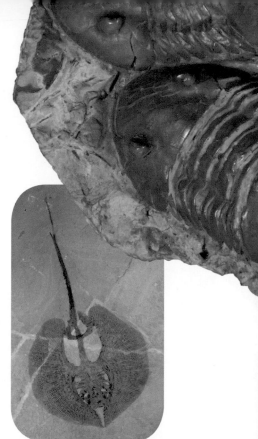

The bones of a fossil stingray. Stingrays still swim in the sea today.

A very old kind of fish, the paddlefish still exists today.

These weird creatures are fossil trilobites. Once very common, they are all extinct (gone) today.

These ancient ferns were trapped in mud.

This isn't a leaf, it's actually a fossil feather from an ancient bird!

This large fossil turtle shell is still attached to rock.

Look at how this fossil branch of a sequoia tree looks almost exactly like a branch from a living sequoia!

FOSSILS, THEN AND NOW

One of the most amazing things about fossils is just how much they can tell us about ancient life. The best fossils are incredibly lifelike and can tell us a great deal about the plant or animal that produced them.

Ichthyosaur (say it "ick-thee-oh-sor") may look like a dolphin, but it was an ancient reptile that lived in the ocean and ate fish.

The extinct pterosaur (say it "tear-oh-soar") wasn't a dinosaur. It was a flying reptile. Even though they look sort of like birds, they were very different.

ABOUT ROCKS

But how did ancient plants and animal bones get trapped in rocks? And how did they turn into minerals? Well, it didn't happen quickly! To understand fossils, it helps to know about rocks, especially sedimentary rocks: the kinds of rocks fossils are found in.

Rocks are the hard materials that make up the surface of the Earth. You walk on many kinds of rocks every day. But there are only three groups of rocks—igneous, metamorphic, and sedimentary. **Igneous rocks** form when hot, melted rock from inside the earth cools off and hardens. **Metamorphic rocks** form when older rocks are heated up and squished deep inside the Earth, changing them into new rocks. But igneous rocks never have fossils, and metamorphic rocks only have them very rarely!

IGNEOUS ROCKS

Igneous rocks, like the granite on the left and the basalt on the right, form when hot melted rock (which comes from deep inside the Earth) cools off and hardens.

Don't bother looking for fossils in hard, tough rocks, like this granite.

METAMORPHIC ROCKS

Metamorphic rocks, like this gneiss (say it "nice") and schist, form when older rocks are squished and heated inside the Earth, changing them into new kinds of rocks.

You'll almost never find fossils in the hard, tight layers of metamorphic rocks.

SEDIMENTARY ROCKS

If you want to find fossils, look for **sedimentary rocks**, which form when sediments stick together. **Sediments** are particles (tiny pieces) of stuff, like sand or mud. Sediments often form when rocks break down in the weather, like when rain or ice breaks little pieces off of rocks. But sediments can also be made of other things, such as the skeletons of tiny animals.

Most sediments are so tiny that water moves them around easily. When lots of sediments **settle**, or sink, to the bottom of lakes and seas, they can make thick, flat layers called **beds**. As more and more heavy sediment builds up, it squashes the sediment below, making the lower sediment beds start to stick together and harden. Over time, they become a solid sedimentary rock. Different kinds of sediments make different kinds of sedimentary rocks!

This photo was taken with a microscope. It shows a jumble of tiny diatoms, little animals too small to see without magnification. Their skeletons are made of minerals, and when they die, they become a kind of sediment, too!

Sand is a common type of sediment. It is made up of tiny grains of broken rocks and minerals.

When sediment like sand or mud flows into a lake or sea, it settles to the bottom and begins to build up.

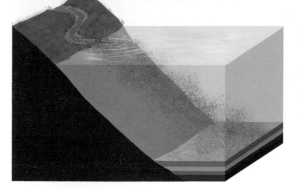

Over long periods of time, the sediment builds up in layers. Some are thicker than others, depending on things like weather and amount of rain.

Eventually, lots of layers build up. The layers at the bottom get squished by all the weight on top of them and begin to compact and harden, becoming sedimentary rock.

Sedimentary rocks form in layers, called beds, as sediment settles year after year. These cliffs are in England. See all the layers? There are lots of fossils in between them!

This shale cliff (left) and these amazing sandstone hills (below) show just how many layers can form in sedimentary rocks.

These are just a few examples of how some sedimentary rocks formed. Sedimentary rocks, such as sandstone, limestone, and shale, are almost always the only kinds of rocks that have fossils in them.

Sand that settled at the bottom of ancient lakes eventually hardened together to form sandstone.

Reefs in ancient seas compacted together and hardened to form limestone.

Mud settled in calm ancient seas and compacted and hardened to form shale.

MINERALS

All rocks, including sedimentary rocks and fossils, have minerals in them. **Minerals** are special chemicals that have hardened. There are lots of different minerals, and each one is made of a different combination of natural chemicals. Deep inside the earth where it is very hot, minerals can **dissolve**, or disappear, into hot water. When that water moves around and cools off, the minerals dissolved in it are left behind and they harden again. As minerals harden, they become **crystals**, and each mineral makes a crystal of a different shape.

Quartz (say it "kwarts") is the most common mineral on Earth's surface. It can form beautiful glassy, pointed crystals.

Quartz can also form as tiny crystals inside the cavities, or holes, in rock. It got there when water with quartz in it flowed into the holes and cooled off.

Rocks and minerals are very different. Minerals are made of a specific chemical combination, but rocks are made up of a mixture of different minerals. Minerals are the building blocks of rocks. Without minerals, there would be no rocks—and no fossils!

You can easily find quartz in rivers and on beaches as white pebbles.

This is a rock called granite; most of the white stuff in it is quartz, but it contains a mixture of other minerals, too, making it a rock.

This piece of fossil wood is quartz, too! Quartz got into the wood as it was fossilizing. It is colorful because there are other minerals in it, too.

HOW DO BONES AND PLANTS GET INSIDE ROCKS?

Long ago, sediment wasn't the only thing settling on the bottom of lakes and seas. When plants and animals died and sank, they settled in the sediment, too. Over time, the plant and animal remains were buried and became part of the sediment beds. Because they were covered in sediment, air couldn't get to the remains. Animals and plants **decay**, or rot away, when exposed to air and bacteria, but without air, they don't fully decay like they normally would. So the remains stayed inside the sediment for a long time, and when the sediment hardened and turned to rock, the buried plant and animal remains became part of the rock, too.

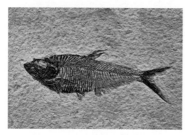

Fossils sometimes give us clues how an animal died. This fish died by itself. Maybe it was sick, or maybe a mudslide buried it quickly.

All of these fish died in one place. Did the water they lived in change? Maybe the pond they lived in dried up?

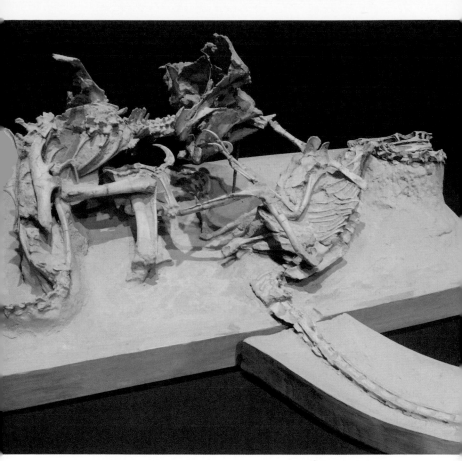

Very rarely, a fossil can show us how two different ancient animals interacted. In this dinosaur fossil, a *Velociraptor* (on the right) and a *Protoceratops* (on the left) died when fighting. The *Velociraptor* had its claws in the *Protoceratops* when they were both buried in a landslide.

HOW MANY FOSSILS FORM

Many fossils formed when dead plants or animals were buried in wet places, like at the bottom of a lake or a bog. Think of a fish in the sea—if it gets buried quickly after it dies, then it's less likely to be eaten by other animals or rot away like it usually would. And if the conditions are just right, it could later become a fossil.

1. When this fish died, it sank to the bottom of the lake. Its soft parts (like its skin and muscles) decayed away, but the hard bones remained.

2. Over time, sediment sank down, burying the bones in a layer of sediment.

Water usually has minerals dissolved in it, and most fossils form when water soaks into the bones and the minerals harden inside. As the sediment around the bones turns to rock, the bones continue to harden with minerals. Plants and animals that have turned into minerals are fossils.

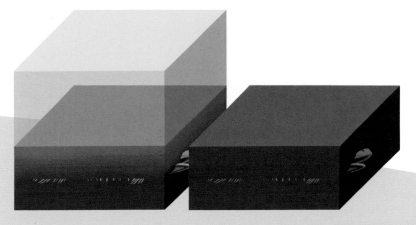

3. After a long time, the bones were completely buried and were squished under the weight of the sediment. Minerals in the water began to soak into the bones, turning them into a fossil.

4. A long time later, when the lake dried up, the sediments all hardened to form rocks and the bones stayed trapped inside the layers.

CELLS AND FOSSILIZATION

Sedimentary rocks form when sediment hardens and sticks together. At the same time, minerals from the ground make their way into the new rock and any plant and animal remains present. But to understand how the bones or tree stumps turn into rocks, you need to understand **cells**.

All plants and animals, including you and me, are made up of tiny things called cells. Cells are like little rooms that hold all of the materials our bodies need to live. There are many different kinds of cells, each with a specific job. For example, the cells in your skin help keep you protected from the sun, and special cells in your bones make blood for your body. Cells are so small that you can't see them without a microscope, but your body has trillions of them! Cells have different jobs in plants, too, like stiff ones to form the stem.

These rounder cells are from a soft part of an animal viewed through a microscope.

These are plant cells through a microscope.

In a microscope, you can still see the rows of cells in this fossilized wood, even though it's millions of years old!

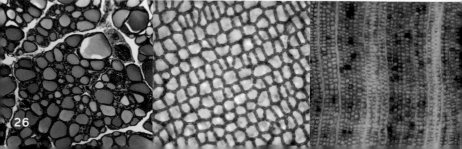

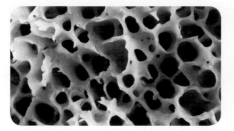

This is the inside of an animal bone. Its compartments make it look like a sponge.

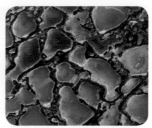

This is a close-up photo of a dinosaur bone fossil. All of the cells are now filled with minerals.

The insides of animal bones are a little bit like a sponge, with lots of little, soft openings. When bones are buried in sediment and water starts to soak in, the minerals in the water can become trapped. When they harden, they fill the cell and copy its shape exactly! Over a long time, when all the cells have been filled with minerals, the bone has turned into a fossil. This is called **fossilization**. In almost all fossils, the original bone is no longer present—it has instead been replaced by minerals in the shape of the bone!

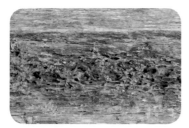

This is a real fossil dinosaur bone. See how the inside still looks spongy? But this bone is now made of minerals!

If you want to get an idea of how bones fossilize, have an adult help you try this: boil some water and dissolve lots of salt in it. Then, after it cools, pour the salty water onto a sponge. In a few days, the salt will crystallize and fill the spaces in the sponge.

1. This shows the cells inside a freshly buried bone. Water that contains minerals starts to soak into the bone's cells and other little openings.

The minerals start to crystallize and fill the little spaces in the bone.

2. After a long time, the cells start to fill in with minerals, and the whole bone starts to turn into rock. This starts from the out-side of the bone and works its way inside.

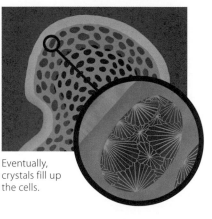

Minerals start to crystallize in the cells.

Eventually, crystals fill up the cells.

Fossils can even preserve tiny details, such as the tiny bones in this lizard foot, or the veins in this leaf.

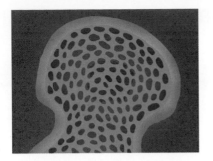

3. Now the bone is almost fully fossil-ized. It takes a long time for all the cells in a bone to turn into minerals. But because this process is slow, it often **preserves**, or keeps, all the tiny details of bone. This also happens with plants, shells, or teeth. When we have lots of little details to study, we can learn a lot more about how the plants and animals used to live.

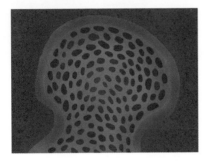

4. Finally, after many, many years, the bone has been completely fossilized. There is no original bone material left, only minerals in the shape of a bone. It is now part of the rock.

While this is one of the main ways that plants and animals can **fossilize**, or turn into fossils, there are a few other ways it happens, too.

OTHER WAYS FOSSILS CAN FORM

Sometimes a bone, shell, or plant inside a sedimentary rock dissolves in water and disappears. Or it may rot away even though it is covered in rock. This can leave behind a hole with the exact shape of the plant or animal remains that were there! Later, other minerals can fill in that gap, taking the shape of the original plant or animal part. This is called a **cast**.

Some plant or animal remains end up being too fragile to last long, but before they disappear, their shape is pressed into the sediment. When the sediment turns to rock, the pressed shape is preserved. This often happens with leaves and other plants or shells. This is called an **impression**, and it shows us the shape of ancient life even though there really isn't a fossil there!

This fossil formed when a tree died and was trapped in rock. As the wood inside disappeared, it left a tree-shaped hole behind. Later, water with minerals in it, such as quartz, filled in the hole and hardened, making a cast of the tree.

This may look like a fossil shell, but it's only the impressed shape of one.

This fly was too fragile to fossilize, but its shape was pressed into the mud when it got buried, preserving its shape in the rock.

Sometimes when an animal or a plant, such as a bug or a leaf, is very soft, thin, or fragile, it doesn't even leave an impression behind. But it can still become a fossil. These fossils are often black and made of carbon, which is a chemical in all living things. When plants and animals are trapped in rock, the carbon is often left behind as a black crust. This is called **carbonization**, and these fossils are very thin layers of carbon on the rock. They're so thin that you could scratch them away with your fingernail. Carbonized fossils look a bit like pictures printed on paper with a rubber stamp.

This is a carbonized leaf fossil.

WHAT ARE FOSSILS MADE OUT OF?

Fossils are made of minerals, and there are thousands of minerals in the world. But only a few minerals are found in fossils. Here are some of the main ones:

Calcite (say it "kal-site") This mineral isn't very tough but it's really common. It forms crystals of many different shapes, including blocks or sharp points. Pure calcite is clear or white, but most isn't pure and it can be other colors. Most fossils have some calcite in them.

Calcite can form as blocky shapes in limestone (left) or as sharp crystal points (right).

This ammonite fossil is made up of crystallized calcite (the calcite is the light-colored material).

Siderite (say it "sidd-er-ite") This mineral is very similar to calcite, but it has iron in it, which makes it browner. It forms crystals in shapes like little blocks or blades. Many fossils contain siderite, especially ones found inside concretions (a special kind of round rock formation, page 39).

Siderite concretions are made up of tiny grains of siderite and can contain fossils inside, like this fern.

Siderite often forms as little blade-shaped crystals, like these, but can also form as small blocks.

Quartz (say it "kwarts") Quartz is one of the most common minerals on Earth! It is hard and usually white or clear. It can form crystals that look like six-sided points. But it can also form as tiny grains that are tightly packed together, which is how it appears in fossils. Fossils made of quartz are hard and can sometimes be very colorful.

Quartz can form long, pointed crystals with six sides, but it is more common as rough chunks. Petrified wood is made up of tiny colorful quartz grains.

Pyrite (say it "pie-rite") This mineral is shiny and metallic. It has the nickname "fool's gold" because of its brassy color, but it has no gold in it. Instead, it contains iron and sulfur, and its crystals look like cubes and are very brittle. Some fossils, especially shells, can be made of pyrite and look like shells made of metal!

Other materials, such as clay or opal, can also be found in fossils.

Pyrite usually forms in perfect cubes. It can also form as chunky masses.

Some fossils, like this brachiopod shell, are entirely pyrite.

35

SEDIMENTARY ROCKS THAT CAN HAVE FOSSILS IN THEM

Because nearly all fossils are found in sedimentary rocks, it helps to learn about the different kinds of sedimentary rocks before you set out to find fossils.

Limestone Corals, clams, and other sea life have hard shells of calcite and other similar minerals; they live together in big layered groups called **reefs**. Limestone is a soft, light-colored rock that formed when old reefs in ancient oceans were buried by new reefs. Over time, they hardened together, becoming limestone. Most limestone actually used to be the bottom of the ocean or a sea! Limestone has lots of calcite in it and can also have lots of fossils of sea creatures. It can feel chalky when you touch it, and if you look closely it can sometimes show lots of little glittery grains. Sometimes it has holes called **vugs**. Most vugs are made by fossils that have dissolved away!

Seashell impression

This vug formed when a fossil dissolved away.

Sandstone Sandstone is just what it sounds like—stone made of sand! When lots of sand settles to the bottom of lakes and seas, minerals dissolved in the water, like calcite, can harden between the grains. This "glues" the sand grains together, making a rock. Most grains of sand are hard little pieces of quartz, so sandstone will often be very rough to the touch. It can also contain fossils, particularly seashells. Sandstone can also be colorful and sometimes has cool layers.

Some sandstone can contain cool fossils, like this crab claw.

Shale Sediments come in all sizes. We think of sand grains as being really small, but some sediments are even smaller, like the tiny sediments in mud or clay. Sediments like these are almost too small to see without a microscope. When lots of these super-tiny sediments settle at the bottom of very calm lakes and seas, they can compact together to form thin layers of rock. When lots of layers build up, it becomes a rock we call shale. Shale is a great rock for fossil collectors because sometimes fossils can be found in between the rock layers! Fish bones, shells, and plants are all common finds in shale. With practice and an adult's help, you can split apart the layers to look for your own shale fossils.

Sometimes, fossils of soft things, such as plants and insects, can be found between shale's layers.

Mudstone Mudstone is a lot like shale. It is made up of very tiny grains of sediment, such as mud or clay, that settled at the bottom of lakes and seas. But the difference between mudstone and shale is that mudstone doesn't have the layers seen in shale. That's because mudstone formed in moving water, but shale formed in calm water. This meant that the sediments couldn't settle into fine layers, like in shale. But mudstone still holds fossils, especially shells.

Fossil crinoid stems are stuck to the rock of this mudstone.

Chert Like limestone, chert is made up of remains of ancient sea life. But chert is made of the skeletons of **diatoms**, which are tiny creatures too small to see. Diatoms have hard skeletons made of a material a lot like quartz, and when they die, their remains sink to the bottom. When lots of their skeletons settle into beds at the ocean bottom, they can turn into quartz and harden together. The result is chert, which is made almost entirely of quartz and is very hard. In certain places, lots of different fossils can be found in chert, including snail shells and algae.

Most chert looks like just a hard rock

This photo, taken from a microscope, shows an example of what diatoms look like.

Conglomerate Sedimentary rocks usually formed in bodies of water, often in calm water. But conglomerate formed in faster-moving water, such as ancient rivers. The flowing water mixed up the sediment, so sand, mud, and even pebbles settled in the same beds. When these sediments hardened, they formed conglomerate, which is a rock made up of lots of different-sized materials. Sometimes you can find fossil shells or teeth hiding between conglomerate's pebbles!

Concretions Concretions are a weird type of rock, and they form in very round shapes. Some are perfect spheres, like marbles, and others may look like funny blobs, but all are rounded without corners. Concretions form inside other sedimentary rocks, like sandstone or shale, as those rocks form. A concretion begins to form when special chemicals form around a plant or animal remain, such as a leaf or a bone. When the chemicals interact with the remains, they harden to form minerals, particularly siderite. This creates a round ball inside the rock, sort of like how a pearl forms in an oyster. This means that sometimes concretions have a fossil at their center! But sometimes other rocks can get worn down and become round, so you'll have to be careful not to get confused when looking for concretions.

Most concretions look like odd, round rocks.

ANCIENT LIFE AND EXTINCTION

The Earth is very old and has had lots of different plants and animals for a long time. Not all of them are still alive today. For billions of years, species have appeared and disappeared. A **species** is a group of similar plants or animals that can reproduce, or make babies. For example, penguins are a bird species, and so are ostriches, but penguins and ostriches can't make babies together. Both are birds, but they are separate species. Some species are much older than others, too. Humans, like you and me, are a young species, we've been around for only about 300,000 years. That may seem like a long time, but some other species have been around for much longer. For example, some species of sturgeon have existed in the world's oceans for more than 100 million years!

Penguins and ostriches are very different species because each adapted (changed) to live better in its environment. Both are birds, but they can't have babies together.

Sometimes when an animal's environment changes a lot, it can't survive. For example, if the Earth warms up or cools off too much, some species die out and disappear. When many animals go extinct at once, it is called an **extinction event**. Extinction events are why some animals, like *T. rex*, aren't around today. Lots of things can cause animals to go extinct, including volcanoes, meteors, and pollution, and we can learn about extinctions long ago by looking at fossils and rocks.

There are many different potential causes for extinctions. Here are a few examples.

ROCK LAYERS TELL A STORY

To understand how and when a fossil plant or animal went extinct, scientists study the rocks that fossils are found in. Rocks form in layers, with younger rocks on top of older rocks. By looking at these layers, scientists can learn how old the rocks are. If a fossil is found in a higher layer, then we know it is younger than a fossil found in a lower layer. And by looking at the different kinds of rocks and fossils in each layer, we can understand what kinds of changes happened on Earth. For example, if a rock layer is very thin, it could mean that it was very dry when it formed. Rock layers are like a history book for the whole Earth.

The Earth's rock layers are a record of how the Earth has changed over time.

1. This *T. rex* skull is the youngest fossil in these rock layers. We know that because it is higher up in the layers and closer to the Earth's surface. If scientists around the world don't find any dinosaurs above the geological layer where the *T. rex* skull was found, we know that dinosaurs went extinct before the next layer formed.

2. This layer is thinner than most of the others. This could be because it formed in a drier era or it formed from a different kind of sediment.

3. This *Triceratops* skull is older than the *T. rex* skull because it is found in a deeper, older layer of rock.

4. This layer is darker and thicker. It may have formed in a wetter time period.

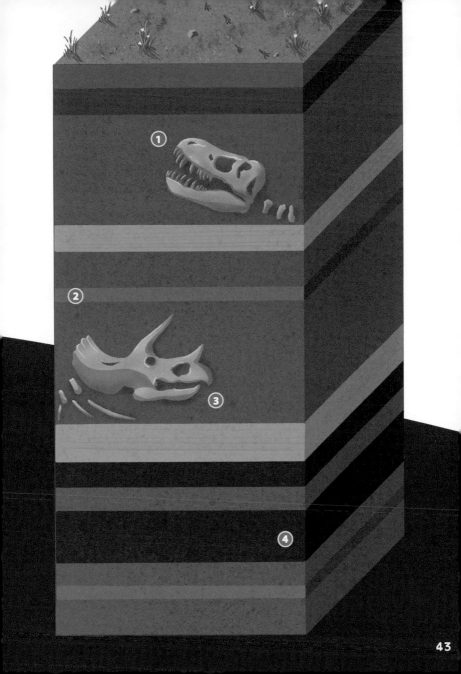

EARTH'S GEOLOGICAL PERIODS
(AND WHEN THEY STARTED)

But Earth's changes don't usually happen quickly. Instead, they happen over millions of years. (Humans haven't even been around for a million years!) To help make sense of this "deep time," scientists divide the history of Earth into different chunks of time, called **geological periods**. The periods have special names; for example, right now we live in a period called the Quaternary. The chart on the next page shows the most important periods and how long ago they began.

At the top of the chart is the most recent period, called the Quaternary period. So far, the Quaternary period hasn't lasted very long, at just over 2 million years. At the bottom of the chart is the Precambrian period. Some periods are much longer than others. The Quaternary is relatively short, but the Cretaceous period (when *T. rex* was alive) lasted 79 million years!

When we find different species of plant and animal fossils, scientists can figure out their age. And by finding similar fossils from different periods, we can see how plants and animals changed over time. When plants and animals **evolve**, or change to better fit in their environment, we can see those changes in their fossils. This is a very important, as it can show us how plants and animals today evolved from species that lived long ago!

Quaternary Period
(started 2.5 million years ago)

Neogene Period
(started 23 million years ago)

Paleogene Period
(started 66 million years ago)

Cretaceous Period
(started 145 million years ago)

Jurassic Period
(started 201 million years ago)

Triassic Period
(started 252 million years ago)

Permian Period
(started 299 million years ago)

Carboniferous Period
(started 359 million years ago)

Devonian Period
(started 419 million years ago)

Silurian Period
(started 443 million years ago)

Ordovician Period
(started 485 million years ago)

Cambrian Period
(started 541 million years ago)

Precambrian Period
(started 4.6 billion years ago)

Today

Modern **humans** appeared around 300,000 years ago.

The first modern **birds** appeared around 121 million years ago.

The first **mammals** appeared around 220 million years ago.

The first **dinosaurs** appeared around 233 million years ago.

The first **land vertebrates** (land animals with spines) appeared around 380 million years ago.

The first **land plants** with roots like today's plants appeared around 390 million years ago.

The first **fish** appeared around 530 million years ago.

The first **animals** of any kind appeared as early as 760 million years ago.

Formation of the Earth
(approximately 4.6 billion years ago)

WHAT IS EVOLUTION?

Evolution is how plants and animals change over long periods of time to better survive in their environment. Over time, plants and animals develop differences from each other. Sometimes these differences can help them survive better, but they also might make it harder for them to survive. These variations are called **mutations**, and they happen naturally. Mutations happen randomly due to natural variations inside plants and animals as they are growing. Mutations are permanent, and they can be passed on to future generations.

To give you an idea of how evolution works, consider this example. If a red butterfly lives in a brown desert, its bright color may make it easier for predators to see and eat it. If the red butterfly survives long enough to lay eggs, most of its babies will also be red butterflies, but sometimes a mutation can happen and make one of the babies a different color. If a mutation makes a butterfly brown, it could more easily hide in a dusty desert. If that brown butterfly grows up to lay eggs, its babies may also be brown. Meanwhile, the red butterflies are eaten by predators. After some

The butterfly on the left has evolved to match this tree perfectly. But the butterfly on the right is brightly colored in a brown desert. Which one do you think will survive longer?

time, the brown butterflies might be the only ones left because they were better at surviving in their environment. As the brown butterflies also develop their own mutations, they can continue to **adapt**, or become better at surviving. Eventually the brown butterflies would be a new species, one that evolved from the red butterfly species.

But not all mutations are helpful. If the brown butterflies had babies with a mutation that made them blue, they'd be easy to spot like the red ones, and they would probably get eaten, too.

When lots of animals are living in one place, the ones with good mutations are often the best at surviving. For example, if lots of different plant-eating animals are the same size, they likely would compete for the same plants. But if one was born with a mutation that made its neck a little longer, it could reach food that was growing higher, and if it got more food, it would have a better chance of surviving. Its babies would likely inherit these longer necks. At the same time, the animals with shorter necks may go hungry because there is too much competition for the low-growing plants.

Evolution happens when good mutations help a plant or animal survive longer than other animals without the same mutations. For example, cheetahs have evolved to be very fast runners in order to hunt fast prey animals, like gazelles. Slower animals are unable to hunt the same fast animals. This means that chee-tahs are better adapted than other predators to survive in areas where fast prey lives.

Mutations aren't the only way that evolution can happen (sometimes, traits are spread when animals or plants migrate from other areas), but they are a major driver of evolution.

You can see examples of evolution when you look at fossils: Sometimes a fossil will show us how one species of animal turned into another over time. These are called **transition fossils**, and they are very helpful to understand how life evolved. For example, fossils of a strange animal called *Archaeopteryx* (say it "ark-ay-op-terr-ix") helped us learn that today's birds evolved directly from dinosaurs. *Archaeopteryx* is a transition fossil in between dinosaurs and birds; it has a skeleton like that of a dinosaur but feathers and wings like a bird!

Both of these shells are from ammonites, which were squid-like sea animals with spiral shells. The ammonite on top is an older species than the one on the bottom. The upper one is thick and rounded, with lots of bumps and ridges. The lower one is a more recent fossil, and you can see it is much smoother and thinner. The smoother one was a better and faster hunter, because its thinner shell allowed it to swim faster than the lumpy one.

For a time, birds and dinosaurs lived side by side, but then a disaster (or more than one) struck, killing the dinosaurs and much of the life on the planet. But birds, thanks to their special adaptations (they were smaller, could fly or glide, and could eat a wide variety of foods), survived. And once the dinosaurs were gone, birds flourished. Today, there are thousands of bird species.

Some people think evolution isn't real, often for religious reasons, but the science is clear: it's happening. One reason people may doubt it is because it happens so slowly (usually over thousands or millions of years) that it's hard to see it in our short lifetimes.

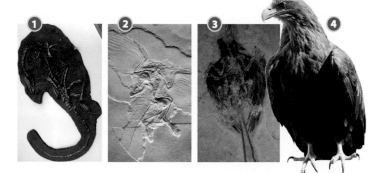

❶ 200 million years ago
This is a fossil of a kind of dinosaur called *Coelophysis* (say it "see-lo-fi-sis"). It had thin bones and tiny feathers, but it had no wings and couldn't fly.

❷ 148 million years ago
This is a fossil of *Archaeopteryx*, which looks a lot like *Coelophysis*, a dinosaur, but it had longer feathers and its arms had begun to evolve into wings.

❸ 131 million years ago
This is a fossil of *Confuciusornis*, an ancient bird that had many feathers and could fly. It is the first bird we know of that had a beak instead of dinosaur-like jaws.

❹ Today
This is an eagle alive today. It is a modern bird. It has long feathers, scaly feet, and a sharp beak with no teeth, and it can fly.

Animal Fossils

There are many different kinds of fossils, from tiny organisms like algae and snails to huge creatures such as giant dinosaurs and entire trees. Let's look at some fossil varieties and how they relate to life today, starting with animal fossils.

Fish are common, but they are still important fossils. Their ones are often finely preserved.

Dinosaurs 52

Reptiles 62

Amphibians 65

Fish 68

Sharks 72

Gastropods 75

Brachiopods and Bivalves 78

Crustaceans 81

Coral and Bryozoans 84

Crinoids and Blastoids 87

Trilobites 90

Ammonites, Baculites, Orthoceras,
Nautilus, and Belemnites 93

Eurypterids 96

Sea Sponges, Algae, and Stromatolites 99

Echinoderms 102

Insects, Arachnids, and Myriapods 105

Mammals 108

A fossil tooth from
an ancient sawfish

Dinosaurs

Dinosaurs are probably the most famous fossils. Complex creatures that first appeared around 233 million years ago in the Triassic period, they were a special kind of reptile that had scaly skin and built nests and laid eggs.

This dinosaur skull is tightly stuck in the rock that preserved it. Most dinosaur fossils are found like this.

When dinosaur fossils were first discovered, they were so strange that they confused scientists, who thought they were finding giant lizard bones, so they named these ancient animals "dinosaurs," which means "terrible lizards." But today we know that dinosaurs were very different from lizards. Lizards are cold-blooded, but some studies suggest that many dinosaurs were warm-blooded, just like birds and people, and we now know that many dinosaurs had feathers, unlike lizards. Some dinosaurs may have been pretty intelligent, too.

Tyrannosaurus rex was one of the most famous dinosaurs.

These illustrations show just three of the many kinds of dinosaurs that once roamed the earth.

Spinosaurus was a huge fish-eating hunter.

Stegosaurus was a plant-eater that could defend itself with its spiked tail.

A plant-eater, *Alamosaurus* was almost 100 feet long!

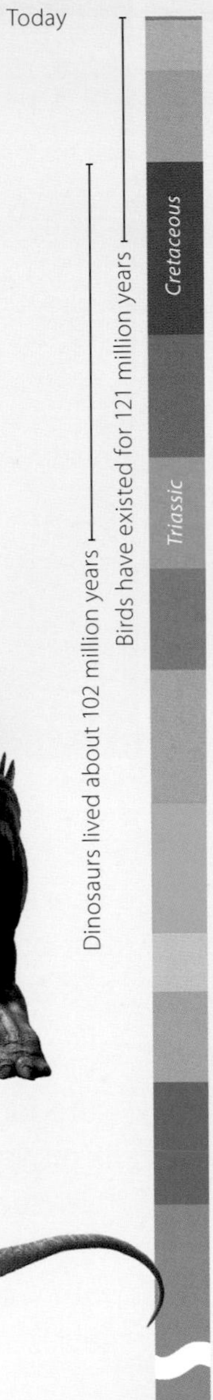

Today

Birds have existed for 121 million years

Dinosaurs lived about 102 million years

Cretaceous

Triassic

Most dinosaur fossils are found like this: a big jumble of bones that must be carefully unburied and pieced back together by scientists.

There were many kinds of dinosaurs. Some were tiny, but others were enormous. Most walked on land and some even could glide through the air.

Scientists have grouped all dinosaurs into two main categories: saurischians (say it "saw-ris-kee-ans") and ornithischians (say it "or-neh-this-kee-ans"). Those may seem like complex words, but they are pretty easy to understand with a few examples. We'll start with saurischians. There are two main groups of saurischians: theropods and sauropods.

Theropods (say it "thair-oh-pods")

Theropods are a group of meat-eating dinosaurs that mostly walked on two legs. They first appeared in the Triassic period, about 233 million years ago, and were the dominant predators when dinosaurs were alive. There were many different theropods, but they didn't all live at the same time. Many of them were probably smart, fast hunters. And thanks to many new fossil discoveries, we know that many theropods, especially the dinosaurs known as raptors, had feathers!

T. rex had a huge head and jaws.

Almost all theropods had sharp teeth for tearing meat.

Raptors were a kind of fast, smart theropod; they were also covered in feathers.

Dilophosaurus was a small theropod that hunted small animals. It had a pair of crests on its head, and might have had feathers, too.

Sauropods (say it "sawr-o-pods")

Also belonging to the saurischian category, sauropods were a group of large dinosaurs that walked on four legs and had very long necks, long tails, and small heads. They ate plants, and most lived in herds. They first appeared in the Triassic period, about 233 million years ago, and were probably the primary prey, or food, that theropods hunted. Sauropods were the largest animals to ever walk on land, and some were almost 100 feet long and weighed over 80 tons— that's the weight of over 6 school buses!

This illustration shows how huge some sauropods, like this *Diplodocus*, were. It towered over the landscape.

The sauropods were huge! *Apatosaurus* was often over 70 feet long.

Sauropods were huge and heavy; these preserved tracks show them sinking into mud.

Sauropods had long, strong necks.

Triceratops were fascinating ornithischians with a big bone frill on their head and three horns, probably for defense.

Ornithischians

Ornithischians were a complex group of dinosaurs and included several different families. They often had unique features, like large horns, club-like tails, or thick armor. Some walked on two legs and others on four, and most ate plants. Many ornithischians probably lived in herds. They first appeared during the Jurassic period, about 200 million years ago.

This might be what a living *Triceratops* looked like.

Stegosaurus was a unique ornithischian. It had a spiked tail to defend itself and bony plates on its back. The plates may have been used as a display.

This *Parasaurolophus* had a crest on its head that made it easy to spot, and it probably could be used to make calls, almost like a trumpet.

This is a fossilized nest of *Hadrosaurus* eggs.

Can I find dinosaur fossils?

Unfortunately, most dinosaur fossils are very rare and you probably won't find them. Even if you did find a dinosaur fossil, you aren't allowed to collect it without first notifying authorities. That's because dinosaur fossils are important and need to be studied! Many are found in Colorado, Oklahoma, and other western and southwestern states, and most specimens are just fragments. But fossils of teeth, broken bones, and even egg shells are not rare, if a scientist is looking in the right place.

This is a piece of a *Spinosaurus* tooth; they ate fish.

Sometimes the spaces inside a dinosaur bone become filled with a special kind of quartz that is very colorful.

This broken dinosaur bone fragment shows the spongy inside of the bone.

These are broken fragments of a dinosaur egg shell.

When did they live? Are they alive today?

The first dinosaurs appeared in the Triassic period, about 233 million years ago. As a group, dinosaurs evolved and adapted for more than 160 million years. Some of the most familiar dinosaurs, such as *Stegosaurus* and *Tyrannosaurus rex*, lived at different times and never met. At the end of the Cretaceous period, about 66 million years ago, almost all dinosaurs went extinct. Many scientists think a huge asteroid (a big space rock) hit the Earth. Others think volcanoes played a role.

A large asteroid likely hit the Earth 66 million years ago.

Either would produce a lot of dust, blocking sunlight and cooling the Earth. This would have killed plants, and the plant-eating dinosaurs would have starved; eventually the meat-eating dinosaurs starved too.

But not *all* dinosaurs went extinct. Some dinosaurs are still alive today: birds! Birds evolved directly from theropod dinosaurs, and they are related to dinosaurs like *T. rex*! For example, bird skeletons and dinosaur skeletons are very similar, and many dinosaur fossils show evidence of feathers. After the dinosaurs died out, birds evolved and diversified. So the next time you see a crow or a chicken, keep in mind that you're looking at a distant descendant of a *T. rex*!

Fossil feathers are an incredible part of dinosaur evolution.

Reptiles

What are they?

Reptiles are cold-blooded animals that have bones and hard scaly skin. They usually have four legs (except snakes, which don't have any), many have a tail, and almost all hatch from eggs. They live in many kinds of environments, including deserts and forests. Some reptiles can run on land, others swim in the oceans, and many have different defenses, like hard shells or claws. Lizards, alligators, crocodiles, turtles, snakes, and geckos are all examples of reptiles, but there were many more kinds of them long ago. Many ancient reptiles were very large and ruled the land and sea even after the dinosaurs evolved. Mosasaurs and plesiosaurs are extinct now, but they are two examples of huge swimming reptiles that were good hunters. Many people think they were dinosaurs because they were so big, but in fact many ancient reptiles were bigger than some dinosaurs!

Mosasaurs were huge reptiles that lived in the oceans. They were fast hunters that ate anything smaller than them. The illustration above shows what they probably looked like.

What are their fossils like?

Reptile fossils come in all shapes and sizes, from enormous bones of ancient alligators to the tiny skeletons of little lizards. But not many reptile fossils are found as entire skeletons. Most are just little parts of their bodies, especially teeth. Some, like mosasaur teeth, are very common, which tells us that there were a lot of them alive long ago. When we do find whole fossil skeletons, it can tell us a lot about that reptile and how it lived. Some had flippers to swim with, and others had hard shells for protection. Some, like pterosaurs, could even fly! In some very well-preserved fossils, we can even see the impression of scales in the rock or remains of food in their stomachs!

Can I find reptile fossils?

Reptile fossils are very rare and hard to find unless you dig in just the right kind of rocks, and it is actually illegal in most states to collect a reptile fossil because they are very important to science and we can learn a lot from them. Reptile fossils are found all over the world, especially in China, but in the United States they have been found in Wyoming, South Dakota, and other states.

Today

Reptiles have existed for 312 million years

Carboniferous

When did they live? Are they still alive today?

Reptiles first appeared in the later part of the Carboniferous period, around 312 million years ago, and many kinds of reptiles are still alive today! Many huge ancient reptiles lived alongside dinosaurs and probably competed with them for food and territory. Some reptiles that are still alive, such as alligators, look almost exactly the same as they did during the time of the dinosaurs! Sometimes animals like this are called "living fossils" because they look just like the fossil alligators we find in rocks. This means that the alligator's adaptations have worked well. Many other reptiles today are also similar to the reptiles we find in fossils.

Reptiles alive today look a lot like the fossil ones we find.

This tiny reptile called a hyphalosaur (say it "hi-fal-oh-sawr") used to live in ponds and lakes.

Amphibians

What are they?

Amphibians are cold-blooded animals that usually have four legs, bones, and soft skin, and that spend much of their lives in water. They hatch from eggs in water and begin life as small larvae. Just as caterpillars turn into butterflies when they grow up, an amphibian larva changes and grows into a very different adult. These larvae, such as tadpoles, have gills and can breathe in the water, but when they become an adult, they form lungs that let them breathe air. Other amphibians include toads and newts. Most amphibians live near water or other wet areas and must lay their eggs in water. And while they may look a lot like reptiles, they are very different, and much older. Amphibians evolved long before reptiles and in fact were among the first vertebrate animals to live on dry land!

What are their fossils like?

There are many kinds of extinct amphibians that can be found in rocks. Some of them were enormous and many feet long, while others were tiny. Amphibian fossils often look like reptiles, with backbones, tails, and four legs, but many ancient amphibians had wide triangle-shaped skulls. Sometimes their skull was wider than the rest of their body!

Amphibians have existed for 370 million years

Devonian

These wide heads can help you tell the difference between an amphibian fossil and that of a reptile. Many ancient amphibians also had short, stubby legs and short tails.

Can I find amphibian fossils?

Unfortunately, amphibian fossils are rare in most places, and even if you found one, it would be illegal to collect it. That's because fossil amphibians are very important to scientists, and each fossil can help us figure out how they lived long ago. Most of the best amphibian fossils come from Europe and Asia, but some have been found in the United States in Wyoming, Ohio, and other states.

When did they live? Are they still alive today?

Amphibians evolved in the later part of the Devonian period, around 370 million years ago. They evolved from lobe-finned fish (page 68), which were ancient fish with little legs attached to their fins. And there were once many kinds of amphibians on earth. In fact, they used to rule the land long before the dinosaurs! But many went extinct after a huge extinction event that happened around 252 million years ago. After that, reptiles began to take over. Today, our most common amphibians are frogs and toads, but there are other varieties still around, including salamanders and newts. Amphibians are found in lakes, ponds, and forests around the world.

This fossil amphibian shows how huge and heavy their heads were. Look at how big the head was compared to the rest of the body!

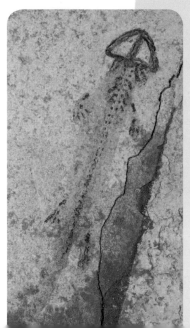

This giant Chinese salamander is one of the biggest kinds of amphibians still alive today. Long ago, however, they got much bigger!

This tiny amphibian fossil is very old. It lived around 280 million years ago. Its big, heavy triangular skull is how you can tell it was an amphibian.

This frog fossil looks just like the frogs alive today.

Fish

What are they?

Fish are animals
that live in water
and that have fins,
scales, and bones, including a backbone and a skull.
(Sharks and rays are a special kind of fish; page 72.)
They breathe using gills that pull air out of the water,
and they can live in fresh water or salt water. They are
also very ancient animals! Fish lived in the oceans long
before any animals lived on land. There are thousands
of different kinds of fish today, but long ago there
were even more kinds of fish, including some really
strange kinds that are mostly long extinct. Here are
some examples:

Jawless fish

The jawless fish were the first fish,
and as you might have guessed,
they didn't have a bottom jaw.
Instead, they had round mouths,
often with lots of teeth, and long,
thin bodies and short fins.

Lampreys are one of the only
living jawless fish left today.

Lobe-finned fish

Lobe-finned fish are almost completely extinct today.
Odd creatures, they had short little limbs, called lobes,
which were almost like small legs. Their fins are on
the ends of the lobes. This is different from most
fish today, which have fins that are attached right to
their bodies, with no limbs in between. As lobe-finned

fish continued to evolve, their lobes turned into legs, and eventually they evolved into amphibians that walked on land!

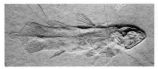
This is a fossil of a lobe-finned fish called a coelacanth.

This is a coelacanth today. Still alive today, they look just like their fossils!

Armored fish

The armored fish, also called placoderms, were big, strong fish that had very hard heads! With bony plates on their heads and backs, they had natural armor to defend themselves from predators. Armored fish are completely extinct today, and we only know about them from fossils.

Armored fish like this, known as placoderms, are extinct.

Some placoderms were huge! This huge skull is in a museum.

Today

Fish have existed for 530 million years

Cambrian

Ray-finned fish

Ray-finned fish are the kinds of fish you are familiar with. They come in all different sizes and shapes, but all of them have fins that are connected directly to their bodies. They are called ray-finned fish because the bones in their fins look like the rays of the sun. From trout to tuna, almost every fish on Earth today is a ray-finned fish!

What are their fossils like?

Fish fossils are found all over the world, and often their bones are very well preserved. Some rocks, like shale, can have entire fish skeletons hidden between the layers in the rock. In many of the best examples, you can see their backbone, their tiny fin bones, and even teeth!

Sometimes lots of fish died all at once and fossilized together. These fossils can help us learn how they died!

Can I find fish fossils?

Fish fossils are not very rare, but they usually take a lot of effort to find. And many states have strict laws that stop you from collecting fossils of animals that have a backbone, and this includes fish. If you find a fish fossil, you should report it to authorities so that it can be properly studied. That way you can help us learn more about the ancient world! Many fish fossils are found in Wyoming, Colorado, and other western states.

Small ray-finned fish fossils like this are common.

When did they live? Are they alive today?

There many kinds of fish alive today in lakes, rivers, and oceans all over the world, but almost all of them are ray-finned fish. Placoderms, the armored fish, are long extinct, and only two types of jawless fish are still alive today: lampreys and hagfish. Similarly, there are only two kinds of lobe-finned fish still alive today, the lungfish and the coelacanths (say it "see-lo-kanths"), which were only recently discovered! The jawless fish first appeared in the oceans in the Cambrian period around 530 million years ago, while most of the other fish appeared in the Devonian period around 419 million years ago. Most of the fish you've ever seen (or eaten) are ray-finned fish, and they are a very successful group of animals because they've adapted to fit into many of the environments on Earth.

Many ancient ray-finned fish looked a lot like modern fish. Look at the similarities between this fossil and this bluegill!

Sharks

What are they?

Sharks are special kinds of fish that don't have regular bones. Instead, their skeletons are made of cartilage, which is the same firm, flexible stuff that your ears and nose are made of! Many sharks are known for being fast and fierce and especially for eating other fish. Like fish, sharks have fins, but they aren't covered in scales. Instead, sharks have a special kind of skin. There are many kinds of sharks and they live in all of the oceans.

What are their fossils like?

Since the softer parts of animals (including a shark's cartilage) don't turn into fossils very easily, most fossils of ancient sharks are just their hard teeth. But we can learn a lot from their teeth, like what kinds of animals they ate and how big the sharks were. For example, we know from fossil teeth that a species called *megalodon* once lived in the oceans, was bigger than a school bus, and ate whales!

Can I find shark fossils?

Yes! Ancient shark teeth are not rare and can be found all over the world. (They are the only vertebrate teeth that are usually legal to collect.) Sometimes they can be found loose in rivers, but they can also be found stuck in rocks. The rivers and beaches of Florida and Georgia are famous for their fossil shark teeth.

When did they live? Are they alive today?

Sharks are very ancient animals. They first appeared in the Silurian period 425 million years ago, and they are still found in the oceans today. Sharks are very successful animals, and they have been able to survive millions of years by adapting to live in all kinds of water and conditions. They are also very good hunters and are at the top of their food chain, which means that no other animal eats them (except people). We can study the sharks in oceans today to learn about how ancient sharks once lived.

A collector is using a special basket to search for fossil shark teeth on a Florida beach.

Today

Sharks have existed for 425 million years

Silurian

These are all fossil shark teeth. Just like other animals, size and shape vary by species. Tooth shape can help scientists learn a lot about the shark.

Megalodon was a type of enormous shark that lived until around 4 million years ago. This coin should give you an idea of how big this tooth is. And this isn't even as big as they can be! *Megalodon* teeth can be found in rivers and beaches in the southeastern United States today.

A large, cone-shaped snail shell

Gastropods

What are they?

Gastropods are a group of small, soft animals that have no bones. Common examples include snails and slugs. Snails have hard shells on their backs, but slugs don't. Most snail shells have some kind of coiled or spiral shape, and many can pull their soft parts into their shells for protection. Some gastropods live on land, but most live in water, especially in salt water.

What are their fossils like?

When we find fossil gastropods, we usually only find their shells. That's because the bodies of slugs and snails were too soft to be preserved in rock, and only the snail shells survived. You won't find fossil slugs because they didn't have any hard parts. But snail shell fossils are very common and are easy to find in several different kinds of rocks! Limestone, sandstone, shale, and chert can all contain snail shells, large and small.

Today

Gastropods have existed for 490 million years or more

Cambrian

Sometimes when they are broken, they just look like little curved pieces stuck in the rock, but those pieces can indicate that you're looking in the right place to find a whole shell!

Can I find gastropod fossils?

Yes, you can! Gastropods, especially snails, are some of the most common fossils you can find. If you look hard enough in rocks like chert or limestone, you might find little coiled shells. They can be found all over the country, especially in the Midwest states of Iowa, Wisconsin, and Illinois, and in the Northeast.

When did they live? Are they alive today?

Gastropods are a very old group of animals that first evolved at least 490 million years ago as sea snails, and they are still alive today. They have lived for so long because they are good at adapting to live in many different kinds of places and to behave in many different ways. In fact, they are so good at adapting that over 60,000 different kinds of gastropods are alive today! You've probably even seen them yourself: slugs in your yard or snails in a pond.

Spiral snail shells come in all sizes. You'll find them in limestone and chert.

Sometimes snail shells can be found flattened in shale.

A large coiled sea snail shell fossil

Some sea snail fossils have more complex shapes, like this pointed one.

Land snails and sea snails, like this one, are still alive today.

Brachiopods and Bivalves
What are they?

Brachiopods and bivalves are two different kinds of shelled mollusks that live at the bottom of oceans and lakes. Like slugs and snails (which also are mollusks) brachiopods and bivalves are soft animals with no bones, and some grow shells for protection. Brachiopods and bivalves both have two-part shells that are joined at a hinge, so they can open and close to protect the soft animal inside. But even though they look a lot alike, they are different kinds of animals. The two halves of a brachiopod shell are shaped differently from each other, and they can anchor themselves with a special kind of a "foot." Bivalves, such as clams and oysters, have shells with two parts that are identical, and they push themselves along the seafloor.

What are their fossils like?

Like lots of other shelled sea creatures, when we find fossils of brachiopods and bivalves, we usually only find their shells. That's because their soft bodies easily rotted away while their hard shells got buried. The two halves of their shells can sometimes be found still together, but more often than not, they

A large fossil clam

are separated. Each half of a bivalve shell is shaped like a scoop. Brachiopod shells can have more unusual shapes, sometimes looking like they have horns, and one half of the shell is usually flatter than the other. Well-preserved shell fossils still look a lot like they did when the animal was alive, but they are almost always embedded in rocks like sandstone or shale.

Can I find brachiopod and bivalve fossils?

Yes, you can! The shells of brachiopods and bivalves are very common fossils. They turn up in several kinds of rocks, especially sandstone, shale, and limestone. Sometimes so many animals died in the same place that you can find rocks with countless pieces of shells in them. Most of the time, you won't find whole fossils, just little pieces of them. In that case, they look like little curved light-colored shapes in the rock. If you have an adult help you break the rock very carefully, you might find more shells inside! On the Pacific Coast, especially in Oregon, you can find whole shells hidden in sandstone.

When did they live? Are they alive today?

Brachiopods and bivalves are very old animals, and have lived in the Earth's oceans and lakes since the Cambrian period, around 540 million years ago! Most brachiopods

Cambrian

Brachiopods and bivalves have existed for at least 540 million years have died out, but bivalves have survived through the ages by being able to adapt to changes in the oceans. You've probably seen bivalves such as clams, oysters, and mussels at the beach, in aquariums, or even in restaurants! They are very common all over the world and are important for the health of lakes, rivers, and seas.

Brachiopods still alive today are very similar to ancient ones. This one is using its long foot to anchor itself on a beach.

A closed fossil clam shell

Fossil brachiopods often have interesting shapes.

These brachiopod shells are attached to limestone.

The most common bivalve and brachiopod fossils look like curved shapes in rock.

Crustaceans (say it "crust-ay-shuns")

What are they?

Crustaceans are a group of animals with hard shells, often multiple pairs of legs, and they usually live in water. Examples include crabs, lobsters, shrimp, and barnacles, and they have been alive in the world's oceans for a very long time. Many crustaceans have ten legs that they use to crawl around the bottoms of oceans and lakes, but others can swim well, too. They all have segmented armor-like bodies, and many also have special arms with pincers or claws that they use to defend themselves and to grab food.

What are their fossils like?

Fossils of crabs, shrimp, and other crustaceans are often well preserved and show the animal's shape, legs, segments, and claws. That's because hard parts of animals fossilize better than soft parts, and most of a crusta-

Barnacles are crustaceans that anchor on rocks. These fossil barnacles look a lot like those living today.

cean's body is made of a hard material that doesn't quickly rot away. And when you see a fossil crab, it may look just like crabs alive

Crustaceans have existed for 511 million years

Cambrian

today! That's because many crustaceans that evolved long ago had become very good at surviving, and they haven't changed much in a very long time. This makes them interesting because we can look at today's crustaceans to figure out how ancient ones lived!

Can I find crustacean fossils?

You might! Most fossils of crustaceans are not very common in the United States, but there are some places where it is possible to find a shrimp fossil or that of another small animal. Sedimentary rocks in Oklahoma and Illinois, for example, hold ancient crustaceans in them. The best fossils will look just like modern shrimp or crabs, but many fossils aren't so clear. Look for segmented shapes that look like armor, or look for crab-like pincers; but don't confuse them for trilobites (page 90).

This is a crab claw embedded in sandstone.

When did they live? Are they alive today?

Crustaceans have been around since the Cambrian period, around 511 million years ago, and they still exist today! Most crustaceans alive today, like lobsters, appeared during the Cretaceous period, which began 145 million years ago, and many dinosaurs and fish likely would have eaten them. The earliest crustaceans were small, strange-looking animals that didn't look much like the ones alive today.

This fossil is the underside of a lobster. Notice all the segments of its hard armor and legs.

The fossil shrimp below looks a lot like shrimp (left) that are alive today. Even its antennae and legs have been preserved.

Corals and Bryozoans (say it "bry-oh-zoh-ans")

What are they?

Corals and bryozoans are tiny animals that live at the bottom of the oceans in big groups called colonies. Each individual coral produces a skeleton, and their colonies, called reefs, are made from many skeletons of these tiny animals! The colonies can't move, so they need the movement of the water to bring food to them. Coral and bryozoan colonies often have lots of branches, and they can almost look like plants, but they are made out of harder materials. But even though their colonies can look a lot alike, corals and bryozoans are actually very different animals.

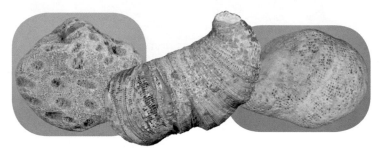

Fossil corals can come in all kinds of shapes, but many have a texture that looks almost like fabric.

What are their fossils like?

Individual corals and bryozoans have hard skeletons, and their colonies are easily preserved in rocks. They are common fossils, especially in limestone. When you find coral or bryozoan fossils they often have very complex patterns with lots of details, and sometimes on coral fossils you can see little circular shapes—those spots are where each little animal used to live!

Can I find coral and bryozoan fossils?

Yes! Corals and bryozoans are very common fossils that can be found all over. They are usually found in limestone, and they turn up in most states, especially in the central United States as well as the Northeast, where there used to be warm seas long ago.

When did they live? Are they alive today?

Both corals and bryozoans are very ancient animals that have been in earth's oceans for millions of years, even before anything lived on land! And they are still alive today in all of the world's oceans. Corals first appeared in the Precambrian period, around 570 million years ago, and bryozoans in the Ordovician period, around 485 million years ago, which makes them among the oldest kinds of animals still alive today.

Many coral fossils look like rocks with strange patterns, like this honeycomb-like pattern.

Today

Ordovician

Precambrian

Bryozoans have existed for 485 million years

Corals have existed for 570 million years

This chert has impressions of fossil coral.

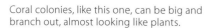

Some bryozoan fossils look weird, like this spiral-shaped bryozoan stem.

Coral colonies, like this one, can be big and branch out, almost looking like plants.

Bryozoans are still alive in the oceans today. They are often confused with coral.

Many bryozoan fossils look like branches in rock.

Crinoids (say it "cry-noids") and Blastoids

What are they?

Crinoids are strange ocean animals you may not have seen before. They have small "heads" shaped like a cup with a ring of tentacles around it, and they often have thick "stems" that anchor them to the seafloor. They look a bit like flowers, which has earned them the nickname "sea lilies," but they are not plants. Their tentacles look feathery and have lots of little "hairs" that help them catch food and bring it down to their mouth. Some kinds of crinoids lose their stems as adults and float through the water. Blastoids are very similar, but they have ball-shaped heads.

What are their fossils like?

The best-preserved crinoid and blastoid fossils show the whole body, from the stem to the tentacles, and they can look like strange flowers in the rock. Sometimes all of their tentacles look tangled together, or they can all be lined up neatly in one direction. But most of the time, when crinoids died, their bodies fell apart, and most fossils are just small pieces, usually parts of the stem. Often many crinoids died in the same area, and today you can find rocks with countless crinoid pieces.

Crinoids have existed for 480 million years

Blastoids existed for 210 million years

Ordovician

Can I find crinoid and blastoid fossils?

Yes! While crinoid heads are uncommon, you can find pieces of their stems very easily. When crinoids died, their stems came apart in little round sections that look like little circles. Some rocks, especially limestone, can have many little crinoid stem fragments within them—they usually look like light-colored circles with a hole at the center. These "Cheerios" can be found all over the United States, especially in the Southwest and the Midwest. Blastoid heads are seen more often than crinoid heads, but they are still uncommon. You'll find their stem segments more often, too.

When did they live? Are they alive today?

Crinoids first appeared in Earth's oceans in the Ordovician period, around 480 million years ago, and have existed ever since. There were many more crinoids long ago than there are today, but they are still found in oceans all over the world. They live primarily in warm-water areas, often in coral reefs. Blastoids first appeared around 472 million years ago, and they went extinct about 251 million years ago.

Some limestone is made up almost entirely of hard crinoid stem fragments!

Ring-shaped fossils like this are little segments of crinoid stems.

This is a "head" of a crinoid. The feathery parts are the tentacles.

A very detailed blastoid head in limestone

Crinoids are a very ancient kind of animal, but they are still alive today! They have long feathery tentacles to catch food.

Crinoid tentacles

These are some blastoid heads on limestone. The ring shape on the left is part of a blastoid stem.

Crinoid "head"

Crinoid stem

Trilobites (say it "try-lo-bite")
What are they?

Trilobites were strange sea creatures that lived on ocean floors long ago. They had oval-shaped, hard-shelled bodies with jointed armor and bulbous heads and tails. They also had antennae (that's the plural of antenna), and many had big eyes to help them find food. Their backs looked a little bit like a washboard, with lots of armor plates, and they could roll up into a ball for defense. Some types even had spikes on their backs. Most trilobites crawled around on the bottoms of oceans where they looked for food in the mud, but some could swim. They were once found in all of the world's oceans but went extinct just before the time of the dinosaurs.

The big curved part at the top of this trilobite is its head.

What are their fossils like?

Fossils of trilobites often appear in shale and other soft sedimentary rocks. They come in the form of whole trilobites as well as fragments of them. When some trilobites died naturally or were eaten by other animals, their hard body parts separated. But when others died and were quickly buried, their bodies stayed in one piece. Today, you'll sometimes find only a head or tail of a trilobite, but sometimes you can find the whole animal. They can also be found curled up in their defensive position! Scientists think many of the curled trilobites died naturally.

Can I find trilobite fossils?

Yes! Trilobites lived for such a long time that countless fossils can be found today all over the world and in different kinds of rocks. Sometimes you'll only find little pieces of their bodies, but whole trilobites can be found, too. Many of the best examples are found in the layers in shale, and many states, such as New York, Ohio, and Wisconsin, are known for nice fossils.

When did they live? Are they alive today?

Trilobites lived in the world's oceans for a very long time, but they are extinct today. They first appeared around 521 million years ago in the Cambrian period, and they lived for an amazing 270 million years! But due to environmental changes, they were not able to survive, and they died out before the Triassic period, so trilobites didn't live during the time of the dinosaurs. Today, we don't really have anything quite like trilobites in our oceans. It is thought that they are most closely related to animals like crustaceans and centipedes, but they are still being studied.

Permian

Cambrian

Trilobites existed for 270 million years

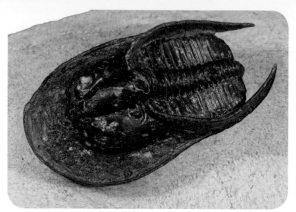

Over time, trilobites developed all kinds of adaptations. This one has a very large head with enough armor to protect its whole body.

Trilobites crawled along the bottom of the ocean to find food and had hard armor and thick heads to protect them.

Some trilobites even evolved spikes as protection from predators.

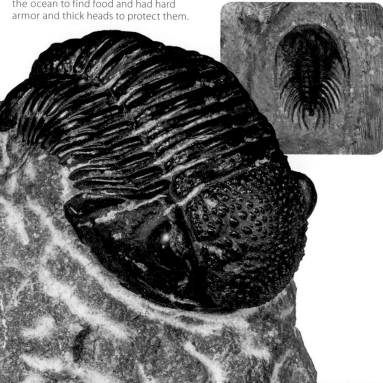

Ammonites, Baculites, Orthoceras, Nautilus, and Belemnites

What are they?

Millions of years ago, there were many different kinds of sea animals that looked like squids, but with hard shells on their backs. Some, like ammonites (say it "ammo-nites") and nautilus (say it "not-ill-us"), had shells that were tightly coiled, or spiraled. But others, like baculites (say it "back-yoo-lites") and orthoceras (say it "or-tho-sair-us") had shells that were straight or slightly curved. Inside their shells, all of them had soft bodies with no bones, and they had tentacles for swimming and catching food. Their hard shells helped protect them, and by controlling the amount of air in their shell, they could rise or dive in the water.

A related kind of animal, called belemnites (say it "bell-em-nites"), were a little different. They were just like a squid but had a tube-shaped skeleton inside them. It is usually the only part of their bodies that fossilized.

Orthoceras had a long straight shell.

This belemnite fossil was actually inside the animal and helped it rise and sink in the water. It was not a shell.

Today

Baculites lived 79 million years

Belemnites lived 168 million years

Nautilus have existed for 250 million years

Ammonites existed for 343 million years

Orthoceras existed for 28 million years

Cretaceous

Triassic

Devonian

Ordovician

What are their fossils like?

When these squid-like animals died, their soft bodies decayed, but their hard shells (and the belemnites' skeletons) did not. If these hard parts got buried, they could easily become preserved in rock. When we find fossils of these animals today, their shells look a lot like they did when they were alive millions of years ago. The shells are made of smaller segments that grew one at a time, and you can often see the separate sections if you look closely. The oldest fossils show shells with smooth connections between the segments, but the younger fossils show shells with very complex connections. Scientists use these differences to help figure out how old the fossils are, as well as how old nearby fossils are, too. Sometimes so many of these animals died in the same place that all of their shells piled up and turned into rocks that are made entirely of shells!

Ammonites were squid-like animals with spiral shells.

Can I find ammonite, baculite, and belemnite fossils?

Yes! Fossils of ammonites, baculites, and belemnites are not very rare, but you'll need to be in the right kind of area in order to find them. The Great Plains states are good places to search. Many very nice examples are found in the Pierre Shale formation, especially in South Dakota and Colorado. Sometimes snail shells can look like ammonite shells, but snail shells are usually smaller and smoother. Orthoceras shells are much older and rarer and generally aren't found in the United States.

When did they live? Are they alive today?

These shelled squid-like animals lived at different periods of time. Orthoceras lived in the Ordovician period, around 470 million years ago, way before the dinosaurs lived. Ammonites first appeared during the Devonian period, around 409 million years ago, and went extinct about 66 million years ago. Baculites lived during the Cretaceous period, which began around 145 million years ago. Today, ammonites, orthoceras, belemnites, and baculites are all extinct, but the oceans are still home to one of their relatives, the nautilus. Nautilus fossils date back 250 million years to the Triassic period, but they are also still alive today! These strange tentacled animals forage for food on the seafloor, and they look like they swim backwards because they put their shells first.

This illustration shows what an ammonite probably looked like. It swam with its shell facing forward, so they looked like they were swimming backwards.

When we cut open ammonite fossils, we can often see the little compartments where it lived.

This straight shell still embedded in rock is a baculite.

Eurypterids (say it "you-rip-ter-ids")
What are they?
Eurypterids were a group of sea creatures that lived a long time ago. They had segmented bodies made of jointed armor plates, two big paddle-like legs for swimming, and several smaller legs for walking on the seafloor. But they also had a sharp, pointed tail, which earned them the nickname of "sea scorpions." They probably used these tails for defense and to help steer when swimming. They were hunters that probably ate fish, trilobites, and anything else smaller than them. Some were ambush predators, which means that they laid still, waiting for prey to come near, and then they quickly attacked!

This nicely preserved eurypterid fossil shows its segmented body, pointy tail, round head, and even its eyes!

What are their fossils like?
Since eurypterids had hard bodies, their segmented shells didn't quickly rot away, and they easily fossilized. This means that when we find eurypterids, the fossils are often fairly complete. Sometimes they are missing some of the legs or the sharp part of the tail, but usually you can see their body segments, head, and

even their eyes. Most eurypterid fossils are just a few inches long, but some rare ones are huge! Scientists have found eurypterids over 7 feet long—that's way taller than the average adult! We have also found eurypterid fossils on every continent, and even examples of eurypterid tracks preserved in rock.

Sometimes we find only parts of a eurypterid, like these broken body segments.

Can I find eurypterid fossils?

Probably not. In the United States, most eurypterid fossils come from New York, and many are from private or pro- tected land. It is possible to find a eurypterid fossil in the Herkimer, New York, area, but unfortunately, it's not likely unless you seek an expert's help.

When did they live? Are they alive today?

Eurypterids first appeared in the oceans during the Ordovician period, around 467 million years ago. They were a successful group of animals that thrived in the seas

Permian

Ordovician

Eurypterids existed for 215 million years

for millions of years. But they went extinct about 252 million years ago. Though they may look a little like crabs, their closest living relatives are actually arachnids, like spiders and scorpions.

This fossil shows the two paddle legs, as well as the "whiskers" at the top of the head, which were actually little feet!

These are the preserved tracks of a eurypterid walking on the seafloor!

An illustration of what a eurypterid may have looked like at the bottom of the ancient sea.

Sea Sponges, Algae, and Stromatolites

What are they?

There are many kinds of living things that don't look like "normal" plants or animals. But many are actually very important.

For example, algae sometimes looks like green slime on rocks or like a plant, but it is actually a different kind of living thing. Kelp, another type of algae, looks like a plant, too. But you've probably never seen a stromatolite before. They look like rounded domes of rock, but stromatolites are actually a kind of bacteria that live in lump-shaped groups in shallow water. And sea sponges can look like a weird plant—you may have seen these at an aquarium—but they are actually an animal that

Stromatolite fossils often look like layered wavy shapes in rocks.

These weird shapes are fossil sea sponges.

Today

Algae has lived at least 1.5 billion years

Stromatolites have lived at least 3.8 billion years

Sponges have existed for 580 million years

Precambrian

has lots of holes in its body, which helps water flow through it. All three of these strange forms of life couldn't move on their own. Instead, water carries them along, bringing them food.

What are their fossils like?

Stromatolites and algae fossils can look just like layers in rock, but they often have a unique wave-like shape or a mushroom shape. Sea sponge fossils usually look like circular groups of small holes in rock, and if the holes are filled in they become difficult to notice. All of these fossils are very common in limestone, and some stromatolites can be found in jasper, where they can be very colorful, often bright red or yellow.

Can I find algae, sea sponge, and stromatolite fossils?

Yes! Fossils of these organisms are very common, but you may not realize you've found one because their fossils are small and easy to overlook. Often, they will just look like swirls, stripes, or wavy shapes in limestone, but these odd shapes will be your clue that you're looking at evidence of ancient life!

These strange little holes in limestone are actually the remains of algae.

When did they live? Are they alive today?

Sea sponges are common in the oceans today, and algae can be found in almost any body of water. Stromatolites are much rarer, and some of the only ones left today are in Australia's Shark Bay. The stromatolites living there are just like the ones we find fossilized in rocks! They may just look like funny rock lumps, but each one is a colony of bacteria, and some colonies alive today are more than 1,000 years old! And these life-forms have been around for a long time; stromatolites first appeared on Earth 3.8 billion years ago! That's 3,800,000,000 years ago!

These dark lumps of rock in the ocean in Australia are living stromatolites.

Rows of wavy lines in rocks are often stromatolite fossils. This rock was cut open, showing you what ancient stromatolites looked like inside.

Sea sponges are still alive in the oceans today. They are a very ancient form of life, older than fish!

Echinoderms (say it "eck-i-noh-derms")

What are they?

The echinoderms are a group of animals that includes many different kinds of ocean life, including starfish, sea cucumbers, sea urchins, and crinoids (page 87).

Most echinoderms live on the seafloor and move very slowly or not at all. Some have many legs, but others have none. You've probably seen a starfish at an aquarium. They have flat bodies with multiple legs and a little mouth underneath. Sea urchins are round, ball-like animals that are covered in sharp

Fossil sea urchins look a lot like living ones. This living urchin has sharp spines.

spikes! Sea cucumbers look like big slugs, but they are often brightly colored and can have spikes, too. And many echinoderms have the amazing ability to regenerate body parts that they've lost, like legs!

What are their fossils like?

Each echinoderm variety left behind different-looking fossils when it died. Starfish fossils look a lot like living starfish! Since they live on the seafloor, they are easily buried by mudslides and other underwater sediment, which means they sometimes are preserved. Sea urchin fossils sometimes look like a jumble of broken needles, since their hard spikes didn't rot away when they died. Sea cucumbers are much rarer as fossils because they have soft bodies. They sometimes just look like flat ovals in the rock.

Can I find echinoderm fossils?

Most echinoderms are rare as fossils, and the only one you'll easily find are little pieces of crinoids (page 87). Crinoids often fell apart when they died, and the segments of their stems are easy to find in limestone today. Look for rocks with little circles in them; the circles often have a round or star-shaped hole at the center. Sometimes so many crinoids all died in one place that the rock can look like it's made up entirely of stem pieces!

These sea urchin fossils are surrounded by lots of their broken spikes.

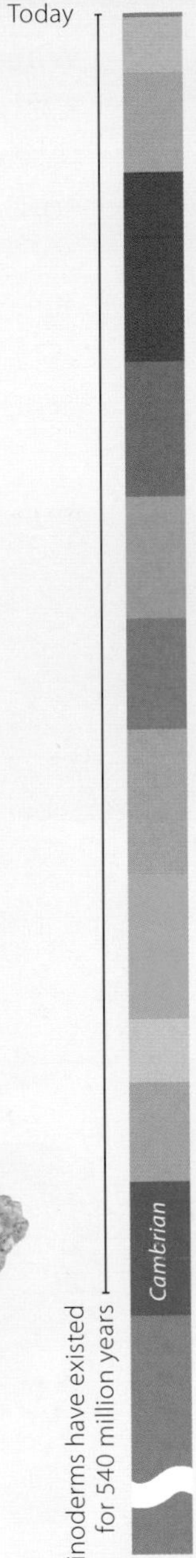

Today

Cambrian

Echinoderms have existed for 540 million years

When did they live? Are they alive today?

Many kinds of echinoderms are still alive in the oceans today, but many more lived long ago. The first echinoderms appeared in the oceans in the Cambrian period, around 540 million years ago! Many kinds of echinoderms evolved over time and have since gone extinct. The echinoderms alive today are actually pretty similar to the echinoderms we find in fossils!

A fossil sea urchin with no spikes attached

The starfish fossils below look just like the ones alive in oceans today.

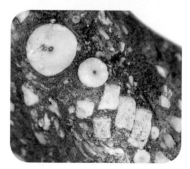

These odd circles in limestone are pieces of stems of crinoids (page 87).

Insects, Arachnids, and Myriapods

What are they?

The animals we call "bugs" are actually different groups of animals. Some are insects, others are arachnids, and still others are myriapods.

Insects are a large group of animals that includes beetles, flies, butterflies, moths, and wasps and bees. All insects have six legs.

A march fly fossil on shale

Arachnids (say it "ah-rak-nids") are a different group of animals; they have eight legs. Famous examples include spiders and scorpions.

Myriapods (say it "meer-ee-a-pods"), such as millipedes and centipedes, are their own group. Myriapods can have hundreds of legs!

Despite their differences, all these "bugs" do have many things in common, such as their segmented bodies and hard exoskeletons (armor-like shells instead of bones). And all of them have been on Earth for a

Today

Arachnids have existed for 390 million years

Myriapods have existed up to 428 million years

Insects have existed for at least 396 million years

Silurian Devonian

This larva (young insect) lived in water, rather than on land.

very long time. In fact, insects, arachnids, and myria-pods were some of the very first creatures to live on dry land!

What are their fossils like?

Even though they have hard exoskeletons, bugs are usually too soft and fragile to be preserved in rock. But it can sometimes happen, especially when they are buried very quickly. In Colorado, for example, there is an area that was once a forest that was buried all at once by ash from a volcano. Sometimes flattened beetles can be found in between the layers of rock there! But more often, bugs decayed away and were not preserved. This makes them rare as fossils. But they can sometimes be found in amber (page 133).

Can I find insect, arachnid, and myriapod fossils?

Probably not. Fossils of insects, arachnids, and myr-iapods are usually very rare. Only certain rocks, such as shale, can have them inside, but fossils are still rare.

Insects, especially water beetles, have been found in natural tar pits, but it isn't safe to collect there.

When did they live? Are they alive today?

Insects, arachnids, and myriapods are all still alive today. The oldest of them are thought to be the myriapods, and they are currently the earliest land-dwelling animals that we know of. Their fossils date back at least to 414 million years ago, and possibly to 428 million years ago. The earliest insect fossils that we have found date back to the Devonian period, around 396 million years ago, but scientists think that insects have been on Earth even longer than that. Most of the earliest bugs were small, crawled on the ground, and ate plants, but flying insects and carnivorous bugs soon evolved. Today, there are millions of different species of insects, arachnids, and myriapods all over the Earth!

A small fossil cockroach

A tiny spider trapped in amber (page 133)

A crane fly preserved in shale compared to a cranefly today.

Mammals

What are they?

Mammals are warm-blooded animals that have fur or hair, and female mammals make milk for their babies. Dogs, cats, horses, pigs, dolphins, and mice are all examples of mammals. Humans, like you and me, are mammals, too! Many mammals are also quite smart. Some of the most famous examples of ancient mammals are large ones like wooly mammoths, mastodons, the *Smilodon* (better known as saber-toothed tigers), the *Glyptodon* (a giant armadillo), giant sloths, giant bears, and giant deer. All of these mammals were larger than most of the mammals alive today, and they lived from around 5 million years ago, with some surviving until just around 4,000 years ago! That means that humans lived alongside some of these animals. In fact, we know that humans hunted wooly mammoths and mastodons!

Glyptodon, often described as a giant armadillo, was a huge mammal with a large hard shell.

What are their fossils like?

Most mammal fossils are much younger than fossils of other animals. That's because there weren't many kinds of mammals until after the dinosaurs went extinct. Some of the bones we have found of mammoths, for example, are as young as 4,000 years old. In fact, some of the remains are so young that they aren't even fossils yet! We can learn a lot about ancient life from mammal fossils because they are often very well preserved. Very old fossils are often flattened because of the weight of the rock they are buried in. But young fossils, like mammals, often have their original shape, and even fur, so we can better understand how they lived and behaved.

Can I find mammal fossils?

You might be able to find mammal fossils if you're in the right place! But collecting them is only allowed for scientists. The rivers in Florida and Georgia sometimes have bones of ancient dolphins and other swimming mammals in them. And many states, like Washington and Ohio, have fossils of animals like wooly mammoths, ancient deer and horses, and even *Smilodon* (the animal popularly known as the saber-tooth tiger)—but they are all very rare.

Mammals have existed for 220 million years

Triassic

When did they live? Are they alive today?

The first mammals evolved from reptiles in the later portion of the Triassic period, around 220 million years ago. The first mammals were small and lived underground in burrows to hide from the much larger reptiles that ruled the land. After the dinosaurs went extinct around 65 million years ago, the small mammals were able to survive. Without the dinosaurs around to eat them, mammals thrived, evolving into many different forms, including some huge animals, like wooly mammoths. Today there are 6,399 species of mammals in almost every type of habitat.

Smilodon, better known as the saber-toothed tiger, is one of the most famous ancient mammals. They lived as recently as 10,000 years ago!

A *Smilodon* attacking a large sloth

This is the flipper of an ancient dolphin.

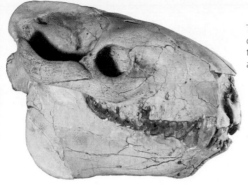

This is the skull of a *Merycoidodon*, a pig-sized animal related to modern-day camels. It lived around 40 million years ago.

This is a fossil skull of a mammal called *Homo erectus*. It was one of our ancestors! It lived around 1 million years ago.

Wooly mammoths were like huge furry elephants. The last ones went extinct only around 4,000 years ago! Ancient people hunted them. This is an illustration of what a wooly mammoth looked like. At the bottom right, you can see a mammoth fossil still in rock.

Plant Fossils and Amber

Fossil plants, like petrified wood and ferns, are common and can be easy to find and identify. But they're also just as important as animal fossils because they give us many clues about what the world and weather were like when they grew.

Ferns and Horsetails 114

Palms 117

Leaves, Stems, and Other Plant Fossils ... 120

Ginkgo Trees 124

Conifers and Pine Cones 127

Petrified Wood......................... 130

Amber 133

Some fossil plants can be quite large, like the long, broken segments of this petrified tree in the Petrified Forest, Arizona.

Ferns and Horsetails

What are they?

Ferns were some of the first plants to live on land. They are special because they don't have seeds or flowers, but instead they grow from tiny spores (seed-like particles) that they release into the air. Ferns grow in clumps that have long stems with broad, flat leaves. Horsetails are a similar kind of plant. They grow long, hollow segmented stems with tiny leaves that grow outward in rings around them. They also grow from spores, not seeds. Both kinds of plants are very ancient, and some that are still growing today have not evolved or changed in millions of years! Both are interesting plants, and there are many kinds alive today, but long ago they were even more common.

Fossil ferns are often found in big masses with lots of leaves all jumbled together. But you can still see how fossil ferns and ferns today look almost the same.

What are their fossils like?

Fossils of ferns and horsetails look a lot like the ones that are alive today. Fossils often show stems and leaves, and sometimes roots. Because both ferns and horsetails were very abundant long ago, many fossils were preserved when they died. Some rocks, like shale, can have so many fossil ferns inside that nearly the whole rock seems to be made of ferns! Some fossils are so well preserved that we can see tiny details on their leaves, which can be used to identify new kinds (species) that we didn't know existed.

Can I find fern and horsetail fossils?

Yes! Fossils of both ferns and horsetails are not rare, if you're in the right area. In Illinois, special rounded rocks called concretions can have fern fossils inside, and sometimes they are very well preserved. Ferns and horsetails can also be found in limestone and shale. Lots of fossil ferns are also found in coal mines, especially in places like Pennsylvania.

Today

Horsetails have existed for 165 million years

Jurassic

Devonian

Ferns have existed for 380 million years

When did they live? Are they alive today?

Ferns first appeared in the later portion of the Devonian period, around 380 million years ago, and some have changed very little since then. Horsetails are a younger kind of plant, and they appeared in Earth's forests in the Jurassic period, around 165 million years ago. The dinosaurs would have lived in and around both kinds of plants, and plant-eating dinosaurs ate them!

These fern fossils were found in concretions, preserving lots of detail.

A fossil horsetail stem in rock

Fossil horsetails look a lot like the ones living today.

Palms

What are they?

Palm trees are an important type of plant that live in warm climates, especially in tropical areas. They can have long trunks that are almost as thick at the bottom as they are at the top, unlike other trees that usually get skinnier toward the top. Palm trees also don't have branches. Instead, at the top of their trunk, there are long clusters of

Fossilized palm wood looks spongy, with lots of little holes. That's because palms, unlike other trees, don't produce growth rings.

leaves, known as fronds. (Sometimes, they are called fans because they look like a fan.) Their wood is soft and spongy, and some palm species are important food plants, providing us with things like coconuts, dates, and other nuts and fruits.

During the time of the dinosaurs, palms were more abundant than they are today. Many grew to be very large, because back then, the planet was warmer, and they could grow in more areas.

What are their fossils like?

Palm fossils look a lot like palms alive today. They often have large fan-shaped leaves with many pointed tips and long stems. Leaves are sometimes several feet long! Rarely, whole palm trees are found as fossils, including the trunk and leaves at the top. This happened when a tree fell and was quickly buried, like in a landslide. Fossilized palm wood looks like a spongy log full of tiny holes or dots. That's because palm wood is different from regular wood and is much softer.

Can I find palm fossils?

It isn't very likely that you'll find a palm fossil in the United States. Some places, like Wyoming, have turned up amazing fossils of huge palm fronds, but they are rare and can only be collected by professionals. You could find a fragment of palm wood in some states, like Texas, but they can be tricky to identify without help.

Many palm fossils look very similar to plants living today.

When did they live? Are they alive today?

Palms appeared in the later portion of the Creta-ceous period, around 80 million years ago, so they are younger than many other kinds of plant. But they still grew and lived alongside some dinosaurs. Palms are still alive today, but they are only found in warm tropical or desert areas with access to water (such as an oasis).

Today, palms live only in warm, wet areas.

This slice of fossilized palm wood shows lots of little dots preserved from the palm's spongy texture.

Fossil palm wood is popular in jewelry. This piece has been cut to be used in a necklace.

Leaves, Stems, and Other Plant Fossils

What are they?

Nearly all trees and shrubs that live on land have leaves, which enable a plant to absorb light from the sun and turn it into energy. Leaves are often thin, soft, and green, with little veins that help move around energy and water. Lots of ancient plants had leaves, too. When leaves fell off and landed in water or mud, they could get buried and trapped in the rock. Since leaves are soft, they easily decayed and rotted away, but sometimes they left an impression behind. As the rock hardened, the impressions hardened, too, and today we can see the shape of ancient leaves left behind in rocks. The same thing often happened with stems and twigs, tree bark, even thorns. Ancient forests were often thick and dense, full of plants that were always dropping leaves and branches. Normally, soft materials like leaves wouldn't easily

Some leaves are preserved so well that you can see all of their details!

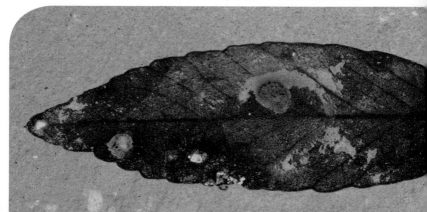

turn into fossils, but since there were so many, there was a better chance of some of them becoming buried and preserved in rock.

What are their fossils like?

The fossil impressions of leaves and twigs look just like leaves and twigs you can find today. Sometimes they are so well preserved that we can even see the veins of the leaves in the rock!

This twig in shale shows leaves and even berries!

These little details help us learn a lot about ancient plants and how they grew. We can also use these details to help figure out which ancient plants are related to plants still growing today. Sometimes this can tell us how warm or wet the world was at the time the fossil leaf was growing.

Can I find plant fossils?

Yes! Fossil leaves, twigs, and even flowers are not rare, and some places will have lots to be found. Most of the best and easiest-to-find fossils

Today

Devonian

Leafy plants have existed for 360 million years

are hidden in between the layers of shale. If you find flaky, layered shale, have an adult use a knife to help you split apart the layers and look for leaves and other fossils. Lots of places around the United States have many leaf fossils to be found, such as in central Colorado, where an entire forest was buried when a volcano erupted, or in Utah and Wyoming, which have ancient, dried-up lakes.

When did they live? Are they alive today?

Ferns (page 114) were some of the first land plants with leaves, and they appeared in the Devonian period, around 380 million years ago. But trees and other plants with leaves first appeared in the Carboniferous period, around 360 million years ago. The trees long ago often didn't look very much like the trees we know today, but they still had woody trunks and could grow very tall. Today, many kinds of leafy plants, including trees, are found all over the world.

Shale's layers are perfect for preserving plant fossils.

This twig has multiple branches and needle-like leaves, details that can help scientists identify it.

Ginkgo Trees

What are they?

The ginkgo tree is a strange kind of plant. They do not have flowers, they grow very slowly, and they have tough, fan-shaped rounded leaves that are different than the leaves of other plants. They are also extremely old plants. The first ginkgoes appeared on Earth long before mammals and dinosaurs were alive. Scientists aren't exactly sure yet how ginkgoes evolved because they are so different from other kinds of plants. But they were common long ago, and their fossils can be found all over the world.

Gingkoes were once much more common than they are today. This petrified gingko log is from the state of Washington, where a forest of fossil gingko trees is found.

What are their fossils like?

Gingko fossils look very much like living gink-goes we find growing today. They are easy to identify thanks to their unusual leaves. Most gingko leaves are shaped like paper fans and have long stems, and in the best-preserved fossils we can even see veins in the leaves. These clear details allow us to compare them to today's gingko trees and have helped us learn a lot about how they grew.

Can I find ginkgo fossils?

It is unlikely that you'll find ginkgo fossils yourself because they are not found in very many places. Washington State and the nearby parts of Canada have produced very nice examples, but they are not found in many other states. Nice fossils must be broken out of rock and are not usually found just lying on the ground.

At first, gingkoes may look like any other tree, until you get close enough to see the strange leaves.

Today

Gingkoes have existed for 270 million years

Permian

When did they live? Are they alive today?

Ginkgo trees first appeared very long ago, in the Permian period around 270 million years ago. There were once several different kinds of ginkgo tree, but today there is only one type alive today, called *Ginkgo biloba*, which is native to China. Today's ginkgo trees are nearly identical to those found 50 million years ago. This makes ginkgo trees very important to study, as they can tell us a lot about the ancient world and how it compares to the world today.

See how the fossil gingko, on the right, is nearly identical to the living gingko leaf today?

Gingko trees are one of the most unique trees on earth.

Conifers and Pine Cones

What are they?

Conifers are trees that usually have needle-like leaves and produce cones. Pine trees are one famous example of conifers: they have sharp needles on their branches and grow pine cones that have seeds inside. These sharp needles are actually special leaves that they use to gather sunlight for energy.

Conifer trees have soft wood and can grow very tall, and their cones can contain many seeds that fall out when the cone opens up. Today, many conifers grow in cooler places, but long ago they grew all over the world.

What are their fossils like?

Conifer fossils, especially their needles, are very common and look a lot like conifers growing today. During the time of the dinosaurs, conifer trees were even more common than they are today, so there are lots of needle fossils that have survived.

Pine cone fossils are rarer but

A flattened pine cone fossil in shale

Today

Conifers have existed for 310 million years

Carboniferous

127

Needles on a twig from an ancient sequoia tree

A twig with sharp needles carbonized in this piece of shale

there are lots of fossils of those, too. Some of the best preserved pine cones still have seeds inside! Most conifer fossils will be found flattened in between the layers of rocks. Because of the carbon and other stuff that conifers are made of, their fossils are often darker than the rock that they are found within.

Can I find conifer fossils?

Yes, you can find conifer fossils. Pine cones are rarer, but pine needles are pretty common in some areas, especially when trapped in rocks like shale. The branches and needles of sequoia trees are especially common in states like Colorado, Wyoming, and many other areas in the western United States.

When did they live? Are they alive today?

The first conifer trees appeared in the late Carboniferous period, around 310 million years ago. Many plant-eating dinosaurs would have eaten conifers as a main source of food! And we still have conifer trees today. Pine, spruce, juniper, and cedars are common examples you can see every day, but redwoods are some of the most impressive. They are the largest trees in the world and can grow over 380 feet tall!

This modern pine cone shares a lot in common with this fossil one (right).

A well-preserved pine cone fragment

This fossil pine cone is broken open to reveal that there are still fossilized seeds inside!

Petrified Wood

What is it?

Petrified wood is the common name for fossilized wood. It is wood from ancient trees that has turned to stone. When trees died and were buried right away, during something like a volcano or a mudslide, they couldn't rot because there wasn't enough air. (Bacteria, which help dead things rot away, often need air to do their job.) When the trees got buried, water in the ground brought minerals to them. As the water got into the wood, minerals began to crystallize in the wood's cells. Eventually, the minerals replaced the wood, turning it to rock. But this happened so slowly that every detail of the wood got preserved, like tree bark, branches, even the grain of the wood.

What are its fossils like?

Petrified wood fossils can look exactly like wood. In some fossils, you can see many details that can tell a lot about the ancient tree, even the growth rings that can tell you how old it was when it died! We can also see the little pores (tiny holes) that helped the tree hold on to water, and we can see tree bark and branches in many pieces of petrified

The bark of this petrified wood is so well preserved it looks just like normal wood!

wood, too. And while all of these things may still look like wood, they're actually made of

stone! Lots of petrified wood can be colorful, depending on the minerals that formed inside the dead tree.

A small fragment of petrified wood as found on an Oregon beach. See the wood grain?

Can I find petrified wood fossils?

Yes, and petrified wood fossils are some of the most common plant fossils that you can find! Lots of petrified wood can be found in desert areas, like in Arizona and Southern California, but it can also be found on beaches, like the Pacific Coast in Oregon and Washington. In fact, petrified wood has been found in almost every state. In most places, the pieces you can find are just small fragments, not whole trees or logs. Sometimes small pieces can look like other rocks, but learning to look for wood grain or growth rings will help identify them. If you want to find petrified wood, look for private ranches that allow visitors to dig (for a price). But don't collect from national parks or state parks!

Triassic

Most petrified wood formed 250 million years ago or less

When did they live? Are they alive today?

Trees first appeared on earth around 359 million years ago, in the Carboniferous period, but most petrified wood is around 250 million years old or younger. That means that when you hold a piece of petrified wood, you may be holding part of a tree that was growing when giant reptiles ruled the earth, or from a tree that grew *before* the dinosaurs! Of course trees are still growing today, and new petrified wood is probably still forming in the right environments.

These colorful pieces of petrified wood are from Arizona.

A stump of a huge tree in Colorado that turned to stone

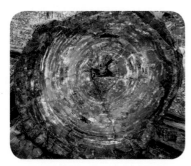

Amber

What is it?

Amber might look like a rock, but it is actually the hardened resin from ancient trees. Resin is the sticky fluid that trees and other plants have inside their wood, and it can sometimes leak out. When ancient trees died and were buried, or when resin that dripped out of a tree was buried, the weight of the earth on top of it caused the resin to start hardening. The hard resin first turns into copal, and after a lot more time in the ground, the copal continues to

You've probably seen resin dripping from a tree like this. If this resin gets buried, it could become amber, too

change and harden to become amber. This means that amber is fossilized tree resin, and because of its color, it is used as a gemstone.

What are its fossils like?

Amber is often yellow or golden brown, sometimes with dark spots, and it is very rough until it is polished. Because resin is very lightweight, amber is, too, and even big chunks aren't very heavy. Some amber is translucent, or see-through, and some is cloudy. But the most amazing thing about

Today

Permian

Amber began forming 300 million years ago

Lots of rough amber, collected on beaches

amber is that sometimes it can have other things trapped inside it, like pieces of tree bark, leaves, flowers, and even whole bugs! This happened when an ancient tree produced sticky resin; when a bug landed on the resin, it got stuck and died. More resin dripped over it and trapped it inside. Over time, the resin hardened and changed, and today, these amazing examples of amber can show us what bugs looked like long ago! Amber is very important because it can trap plants and animals that don't normally fossilize.

Can I find amber fossils?

Probably not. It is very rare in most places around the world, and it is only found in a few places in the United States. Some very rare amber has been found in Arkansas, New Jersey, and Washington.

Amber can range in color from yellow and red to brown and even blue!

134

The world's best amber is found in places like Poland, Russia, Ukraine, and the Dominican Republic—where some rare amber is actually blue!

When did it form?

The oldest amber we know about formed around 300 million years ago, but some is as young as just one million years old. Baltic Amber, from Europe, is the most famous amber, and it formed about 44 million years ago. Copal, which is the softer, less-changed type of hardened resin, is often (but not always) only thousands of years old.

This polished piece of amber has some tiny little bugs inside. See that tiny speck the line is pointing at?

This tiny fly is so well preserved you can see its eyes and wings!

Microfossils, Trace Fossils, Hydrocarbons, Coal, and Pseudofossils

Not all fossils are big dinosaur bones or petrified trees. Many fossils are so tiny that you can't even see them, and others are just the footprints of ancient creatures that once walked through the mud. And some ancient life has even been transformed into materials we use as fuel today! In this section, we'll look at some of these more unusual fossils.

Footprints of giant sauropod dinosaurs preserved in rock

Microfossils 138
Trace Fossils. 141
Hydrocarbons 144
Coal. 147
Pseudofossils 150

Chalk forms at the bottom of seas from countless tiny skeletons of sea life that sank to the bottom. That makes these chalk cliffs like a giant fossil!

Microfossils

What are they?

Microfossils are fossils so tiny that you need a micro-scope to see them! You've probably already held microfossils and didn't even know it. That's because

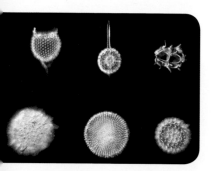

This is a photo of diatoms through a microscope. When lots of them die and settle to the seafloor, they eventually harden to form chert!

many of them look like regular rocks. Some rocks, like chert, have wavy layers in them that were originally formed by algae or bacteria. And some, like chalk, are completely made up of fossils! Chalk is a special kind of limestone, and under a powerful microscope, you can see that it is made up of little round grains that are actually the skeletons of tiny ancient sea life. So many of them died and sank that their skeletons built up into thick layers that hardened to form a rock.

What are their fossils like?

Many microfossils look like rocks. Chert, limestone, and other sedimentary rocks can contain microfossils or be made up entirely of microfossils, but you won't really be able to tell unless you know somebody with a powerful microscope! Microfossils can be hard to identify as fossils because they don't always look like plants or animals, but they are still very scientifically important.

Can I find microfossils?

Yes, you can easily find microfossils! There are many common examples, and they can be found all over the United States, especially along rivers or beaches. The trouble is in identifying them. Because each of the fossils is so tiny, you won't be able to see any of its features. And the rocks they are found in don't look like fossils either. So it helps to understand what kinds of rocks are made up of tiny ancient life forms. Most kinds of chert are made up of skeletons of sea life, and so are some kinds of limestone, especially chalk. Chert is very hard and looks kind of waxy, and it is very common. Chalk is usually white, very soft, and dusty. But most chalkboard chalk today isn't made up of fossils. The chalk used on chalkboards was once made of microfossil chalk, but nowadays it's often made of other materials.

The chert on the left is water-worn. Black chert is called flint.

Cretaceous

Most chalk formed around 100 million years ago

Most chert formed between 2 billion and 400 million years ago

Precambrian

When did they form?

Microfossils formed at different times throughout history. Much of the world's chalk formed during the Cretaceous period, about 100 million years ago. Chert is often much older, often between 400 million years old and 2 billion years old! Chert may look like a boring rock, but next time you pick up a piece, you'll know that it probably contains the remains of some of the oldest life on earth!

This rough chert has wavy lines in it made by bacteria called stromatolites.

A rough chunk of chalk

The famous white cliffs of Dover, England, are made up entirely of chalk.

Trace Fossils
What are they?

Trace fossils are a little unusual. They are fossils left behind by animals, but they don't preserve the animal itself. Dinosaur tracks, animal burrows, and even fossilized poop are examples of trace fossils. For example, when some shellfish, like clams or other small sea creatures move along the seafloor, they can leave tracks in the mud. If the water is very calm, the tracks can be preserved in the mud when it hardens. Today, we can still see these tracks in the rock. Trace fossils are important because they can help us learn about how animals moved and what they ate. And sometimes very soft animals that usually aren't preserved at all leave tracks that can still be found in rocks. Sometimes trace fossils are the only way we know that an animal ever existed!

Dinosaur tracks are some of the most exciting trace fossils!

Today

Cambrian

Some trace fossils can be as old as 540 million years

The strange marks on this shale are the tracks of ancient worms that tunneled through the mud before it hardened.

What are their fossils like?

Most trace fossils are not very noticeable because they are small or just look like part of the surrounding rock. Sea animal tracks may look like little lines or paths in the rock, a groove into the rock, or as a ridge sticking out from the rock. Some animal burrows may look like odd holes or tunnels through rocks. Fossil animal poop is called coprolite and it looks like rocky blobs, but can be very difficult to identify without an expert's help.

This petrified wood has holes in it that were made by wood-eating *Teredo* clams.

Can I find trace fossils?

Yes! Some trace fossils are pretty common, such as the tracks left behind by little sea creatures. These are easiest to find in shale, particularly in states in the Northeast and the Southwest. Other trace fossils, like dinosaur footprints, are important to science because they can tell us a lot about the dinosaur that made them. We can learn things like how fast they moved and if they traveled together or alone.

When did they form?

A trace fossil's age depends on when the creature that made it lived. This could be very long ago, like sea animal tracks from the Cambrian period, 540 million years ago, or mammoth footprints from just 45,000 years ago.

This cut piece of limestone reveals the ancient tunnels of sea cucumbers. Their soft bodies weren't fossilized, but their tunnels were!

This weird rock is called a coprolite—a fancy word for fossil poop! This was probably turtle poop.

Hydrocarbons

What are they?

At first, hydrocarbons don't seem like fossils at all, because most are liquid or gas! Hydrocarbons are made of **hydrogen** and **carbon**, which are elements found in all types of life. They are like "ingredients" that help make plants and animals. When lots of plankton and algae die in one place and can't rot away, such as at the bottom of a deep sea or when they get buried very quickly, they can start to be pressed together by the weight above them. Over time, they are buried deep in the Earth, where they are squashed and heated. The hydrogen and carbon in them start to change, combining to make hydrocarbons. There are many kinds of hydrocarbons, and when we find them they are usually combined together in a mixture we call petroleum. We mine hydrocarbons from deep underground to make gasoline and other fuels that we burn for energy. We call these "fossil fuels" because they're fossils and they're fuels!

These tiny plankton, photographed through a microscope, and this green algae are the two main forms of life that turned into hydrocarbons.

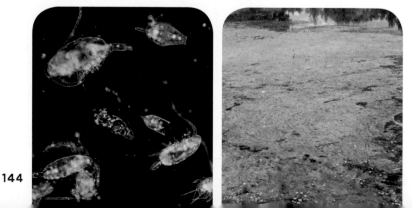

What are its fossils like?

The hydrocarbons we can see usually look like dark brown, thick, sticky liquids. Hydrocarbons that are gasses are usually invisible, but they may have a bad smell. You've probably heard of some hydrocarbons before. There are many different kinds, and each has its own name, such as methane and propane. When we process hydrocarbons in a refinery, we get gasoline and other fuels that we use in our cars and to make electricity.

Can I find hydrocarbon fossils?

You won't usually find hydrocarbons because they form deep underground and are rarely on the Earth's surface. But there are certain kinds of rocks that could have some oil in them. Some geodes, which are hollow rocks that can be broken open to reveal crystals inside, can rarely have oil inside them, particularly ones from parts of Iowa, Illinois, and New York. In a few rare places, a mix of hydrocarbons called tar bubbles up to the surface. Hydrocarbons are a limited resource mined all over the world because we rely on them for power. But burning them also produces carbon dioxide, a gas that makes the Earth warmer and changes the climate (the Earth's weather over a long time).

Most hydrocarbons formed from algae and plankton that lived 359–290 million years ago

Carboniferous

When did it form?

Most hydrocarbons formed from plankton and algae that lived in the Carboniferous period, which began around 359 million years ago. This was a time on Earth when lots of new plants and animals were appearing on land in large numbers, and big forests grew all over the planet. In the oceans and lakes, there was so much plankton and algae that when they died they made thick layers of mud. Over millions of years, that mud slowly changed into hydrocarbons.

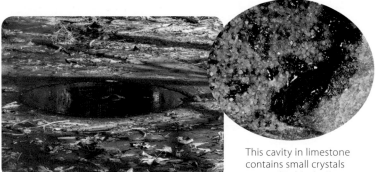

This cavity in limestone contains small crystals covered in black oil.

A natural tar pool in California

Oil is found all over the world, including beneath the oceans.

Coal

What is it?

Coal is a special kind of fossilized plant material that has actually turned into rock. Coal forms when plants in a swampy area died and fell down into the swamp. Over time, more plants died, burying them deeper. Eventually, they formed a material called **peat**. This peat was later pressed together and hardened. All of that pressure, combined with heat from within the earth, turned the wood and plants into coal. Coal also has lots of carbon in it. **Carbon** is an element found in living things, and it can burn. Lots of coal is burned to create electricity, but it creates a lot of pollution, so its popularity is fading. Because coal is a fuel made from fossils, we call it a **fossil fuel**.

Today

Carboniferous

Coal started forming 359 million years ago

147

What are its fossils like?

There are a few different kinds of coal, but most coal looks like a shiny black rock. It is usually lightweight, and even big pieces are easy to lift. Some types of coal have flaky layers and others are more solid, but it is all usually very dirty and will make your hands black if you pick it up. You can't usually see plant shapes in coal, so it can be hard to tell that it once began as a tree or a fern, but this interesting kind of rock is actually an important fossil.

This is a chunk of anthracite, which is a harder, shiny kind of coal that burns well.

This is a softer type of coal, called lignite.

Can I find coal fossils?

It is possible that you could find coal if you're in the right part of United States. Coal can often be found near the Earth's surface, which is what makes it so easy to dig up to use as energy. In places like Pennsylvania, many mountains and hills are made up of large amounts of coal. In other parts of the country, you may not be able to find it anywhere. Look for shiny black rocks that don't weigh very much.

When did it form?

Coal formed in the Carboniferous period, around 359 million years ago. This was a period of major plant growth, and forests covered the planet. The ancient trees were very different from the trees we see growing today (they had much more bark), so they didn't rot away very quickly when they died. As the dead plants got buried, heat and pressure turned them into coal over a very long time. This process isn't quick, though: it takes millions of years for coal to form!

Coal isn't usually pretty, but sometimes you can also find nicely preserved plants in it!

PSEUDOFOSSILS

Sometimes you might mistake an interesting shape in a rock for a bone, or a leaf-like pattern for a plant fossil, but there are lots of rocks and minerals that look like fossils but weren't actually left behind by plants or animals.

These are called pseudofossils (say it "soo-doe-fossils"). The word pseudofossil means "false fossil." Here are a few examples.

Moss agates

Moss agates are a kind of mineral formation that contain squiggles of colorful lines that look a little like moss, lichen, or plant roots. Even though we call these "moss agates," they don't actually contain moss. Instead, they are special growths of minerals that contain iron. Some people confuse these for fossil moss, but now you know better!

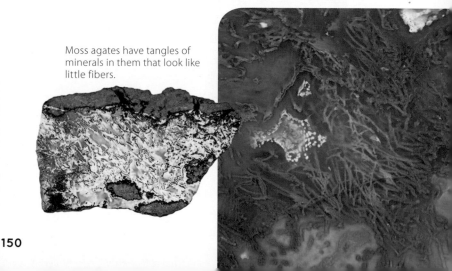

Moss agates have tangles of minerals in them that look like little fibers.

Dendrites

Dendrites are mineral growths that form on the surface of rocks and minerals. They are very thin, and you can often scratch them away with just your

fingernails. Dendrites look like little plants or trees, but they are actually made of minerals containing iron or manganese. They formed a little bit like the way that frost forms on a window in winter.

This looks a little like a fossil fern, but it's a dendrite.

Little dendrites in an agate

Concretions

Concretions are special kinds of rocks that can look like balls or weird blobs. They can look a little bit like bone, but they are actually a kind of sedimentary rock. They form when minerals begin to stick to a small piece of plant or animal material, like a shark tooth or a fern leaf. So concretions themselves are not fossils, but they may have a fossil inside!

Concretions may have formed around a small fossil.

Some concretions can be huge. This one, from New Zealand, is too heavy to lift.

Collecting Fossils

After learning all about fossils and how they formed, you probably want to try to find some of your own! Some fossils are easy to find because they are common. Others, like dinosaurs, are very rare, and because they are important to science, it's against the law to collect them yourself.

Once you've learned about the kinds of sedimentary rocks that may contain fossils, you can start looking for signs of ancient life in the rocks you pick up! Here are some tips for looking for fossils the safe, smart way.

COLLECTING FOSSILS

Can I Collect Fossils Everywhere?........ 154

How Do I Stay Safe When Collecting?..... 156

Where to Look 158

How to Spot Fossils in Nature 162

Signs of Fossils that You Should
Look for................................ 166

How Do You Collect Fossils?............. 168

How Scientists Collect Fossils 170

Identifying Fossils...................... 171

Rock Shops and Buying Fossils 172

Replicas 174

Fake Fossils............................ 174

Fossils of vertebrate animals (animals with
a backbone), like this large lizard fossil, are
illegal to collect except by scientists who
study them.

CAN I COLLECT FOSSILS EVERYWHERE?

Looking for fossils can be fun, especially if you are finding some cool stuff. But it is important to remember that collecting isn't allowed everywhere. Many important places are protected by the local, state, or federal government. This includes national parks, many state parks, and Native American reservations. It is illegal, and wrong, to collect rocks and fossils in these places! You also can't collect anything on private property without getting permission first. Collecting fossils on someone else's land is against the law.

As a general rule, it's important to remember that it is illegal to collect vertebrate fossils—animals that have a backbone (a spine), such as reptiles, fish, or mammals. Vertebrate fossils are rare and important to scientists, and we can learn a lot about ancient life from them. If you find a fossil like this, you should leave it where it is! Take a photo, write down its location, and inform a local school, museum, or other authorities.

If you aren't sure where it's OK to collect fossils, always ask an adult for help. To find land where you can collect invertebrate fossils legally, check your state's natural resources agency or department of natural resources. Fossil collecting is allowed on some federal land, but check the Bureau of Land Management (blm.gov) for details. And you can always check with nearby rock shops or fossil clubs, too.

The good news is that fossils of animals like snails, ammonites, trilobites and coral, as well as those of plants, are usually OK to collect in many places.

Fossil corals, snail shells, and clam shells are popular and common collectibles.

HOW DO I STAY SAFE WHEN FOSSIL COLLECTING?

If you plan to go fossil hunting, **never** go out alone, **never** leave home without a parent or an adult, and **always** tell other people where you're going. Stay safe by following these guidelines:

- Never, ever go out alone. Always ask an adult to come with you.

- Always bring a map, a charged mobile phone, and a GPS system; a mobile phone lets you call for help if you need it.

- Always bring water to drink.

- Never go into rivers, lakes, or oceans; even if the water looks calm, it could be moving very fast.

- Never collect on or near a busy road.

- Never go near cliffs. If you are on top of one, you could fall. If you're below one, rocks could fall on you.

- If a rock or fossil is out of reach, just leave it! Never do anything risky to get a rock.

- Never go onto private property (this means land that someone else owns). If you see signs that say, "no trespassing," turn around right away.

- Always wear gloves when digging in rocks, and wash your hands afterward, and don't touch your face or eyes with dirty hands.

- Always keep an eye out for animals and dangerous plants! This includes everything from snakes and bears to poison ivy and cactus.

What should I bring for fossil collecting?

- An adult!
- Gloves, because some rocks can be sharp
- A small shovel or trowel
- A notebook and a pencil, to write down where you found your fossils
- Water, to drink (and wash off your finds)
- Sunscreen and a hat, to protect your eyes; a hat also makes it easier to see fossils
- Sturdy shoes, to protect your feet from rocks
- A mobile phone, to call for help if you need to
- A map or GPS system so you don't get lost
- Some paper towels, to wrap up fragile specimens
- A magnifying glass, to look at small details
- A backpack for your supplies and discoveries

Are some fossils worth money?

Many common fossils, like coral, snails, and shells, aren't worth much money. But that's OK because it's still cool to find a piece of ancient life! Very rare fossils, like dinosaur teeth and reptile skeletons, can be valuable, but they are almost always illegal to collect. But collecting fossils isn't about money; it's a way to start doing science and to learn about our ancient Earth.

WHERE TO LOOK

In the United States, fossils can be found in every state! Most of the time they are just small fossils of algae or petrified wood, but some states have fish, dinosaurs, and other exciting fossils. But you can't look just anywhere. You'll need to search in the right region and in the right kinds of rocks.

Remember that fossils are only found in sedimentary rocks. Learning to identify and spot sedimentary rocks in nature will help you figure out where you might find fossils. If you are in an area with only dark, heavy, volcanic rocks, you won't want to fossil hunt there, because they aren't found in volcanic rocks. But if you see lots of sandstone, limestone, or other

sedimentary rocks around, you'll know that fossils could be nearby. It will take some practice and more reading to learn about the geology around you, but here are a few tips to help you!

A coral fossil in limestone on a beach

Layered rock formations

Most sedimentary rocks form in layers, and many of the best fossils are found in between the layers. When you see rock formations that have many flat layers, you may be in a good spot to look for fossils. Some sedimentary rocks, like shale, will easily break apart along the layers. You can carefully break apart these layers to look for fossils hiding between them. But remember that other kinds of rocks can form layers, too. Metamorphic and igneous rocks can sometimes have colored layers, but those rocks almost never have fossils. You can tell them apart from sedimentary rocks because metamorphic and igneous rocks often have more speckled color and are harder than most sedimentary rocks.

Soft rocks with lots of holes

Sometimes rocks have odd holes or lots of gaps and spaces in them. In sedimentary rocks, these holes are often made by fossils! In limestone, for example, irregular holes (called vugs) were made by fossils that later dissolved, or washed away. Looking for light-colored rocks with vugs is a good way to find limestone. And you want to find limestone because it can have fossils in it! Not all limestone will have vugs, but keep an eye out for them anyway.

Layered rocks like these are the perfect place to look for fossils.

These limestone boulders have holes where fossils dissolved. But these holes also mean that more fossils are probably nearby!

Some rocks with lots of holes aren't sedimentary and don't have fossils. If you find a dark rock with lots of round holes, it's probably an igneous rock like basalt, which has no fossils.

Exposed rock

It is easiest to find fossils in exposed rock because they don't need to be dug up. Most fossils are easier to find in dry areas or other places where plants don't easily grow. That's because plants like trees and grass will cover up the rocks that may have fossils in them. That makes deserts a great place to look for fossils, because rocks are so easy to find. If you don't live near a desert region, you can look near rivers or beaches where lots of rocks are exposed. Sometimes riverbanks will reveal layered sedimentary rocks full of fossils. But be careful around deserts and rushing water because they can be dangerous!

You won't find fossils in basalt.

This hillside is covered in limestone cobbles full of fossils! Whenever you see soft gray rocks like this, start looking!

Cobble beaches, like this one in Oregon, can often have fossil shells and wood.

Gravel and other loose rocks

If you are on a beach, walking along a river, or even on a rocky road, you can look for fossils. Some fossils, like petrified wood, are often very hard and will wash up on beaches. Other common fossils, like crinoids, can be found loose in gravel if you're in the right area. Not all beaches, rivers, or rocky areas have fossils, but since the loose rock is easy to search through, have a look!

HOW TO SPOT FOSSILS IN NATURE

Even if you have found the right kinds of rocks to look for fossils, how do you know if you've found one? Your first clue is that fossils often look out of place in a rock. The spiral shells of snails or the stems of a crinoid are usually different enough from the rest of the rock that you'll spot them right away. But sometimes they are not so clear. Use this checklist to figure out if you may have found a fossil:

1. Is the rock sedimentary?

Remember what you've learned about sedimentary rocks, especially limestone, shale, chert, and sandstone. With the exception of chert, many of these rocks are soft and made up of tiny grains, and they are often layered.

2. Does the shape you think might be a fossil match the rest of the rock? Are there other shapes like it in the rock?

If you see a strange shape in a sedimentary rock, like a curving line or a little circle, you may have found a fossil! Sometimes sedimentary rocks can have interesting markings, stripes, or shapes that are not fossils, so look carefully at any odd

This sandstone has some interesting swirls and curves. They are the edges of lots of shell fossils.

shapes you find. If they look like they are made of different stuff from the rest of the rock, it's probably a fossil. But also look for more shapes like it. Lots of fossils, especially sea life fossils, are common, and where you find one, you'll probably find many more.

3. Does the shape you think might be a fossil match something alive today?

If you find something in a sedimentary rock that looks like part of a living plant or animal, then you may have found a fossil! Some fossils, like some snail and clam shells, look just like the shells of living ones. If you're not sure if a fossil resembles a living animal, try reading about sea life and other animals around the world.

This long shape in this limestone really stands out. It looks unusual, doesn't it? That's because it's a fossil! It's a long crinoid stem.

4. If it doesn't look like a plant or animal that you know, is there a clear pattern?

Some fossils, like coral or algae, may not look like an life-form that you know, but their fossils often show a pattern that you can learn to spot. For example, coral fossils look like a honey-comb, and some algae look like circles or grids made of little holes. Rocks can have interesting patterns of their own, but in many sedimentary rocks, patterns like these will be a sign of fossils.

Not all fossils will be easy to identify. Some will take lots of research to figure out. In fact, some fossils may be so hard to spot that you might walk right over them without noticing! But keep reading about fossils, and you'll learn about the many kinds of fossils that exist.

This piece of sandstone from a beach has some strange markings on it. Do they look familiar?

The same kind of shapes are seen on this seashell fossil. Could the sandstone above have a shell in it?

Both of the two shells above are scallop shells! Here's a modern one to compare. See how they're almost identical?

You may not know what this is at first, but the pattern of little cup-shaped holes is a clue that it's a fossil! It's a coral fossil.

This piece of fossil coral has a pattern of openings that kind of look like fabric.

This petrified wood is easy to miss, but look for its wood grain.

These strange columns are an interesting pattern and different from the rest of the rock. These are stromatolite fossils!

SIGNS OF FOSSILS THAT YOU SHOULD LOOK FOR

Spotting fossils can be difficult when you've just started. But you can quickly learn how to identify common fossils when you're out hunting for them.

Fossil seashells are pretty common. But sometimes you only see part of them. The curving white shape in this rock is the edge of a clam shell hidden in the rock.

The tube-shaped thing in this rock is part of a crinoid stem. Sometimes they can almost look like bones, but crinoids are much more common than animal bones and are always round on the end.

Sometimes limestone is so full of sea life fossils that it gets a speckled, bumpy look. This rock is made entirely of crinoid stems and broken seashells.

You might see limestone or chert with a wavy pattern of layers; sometimes the pattern is mushroom-shaped. These are signs of stromatolites, which are ancient bacteria and one of the first forms of life on earth!

Sometimes, especially in shale and mudstone, you might see some dark spots or thin black layers in the rock. In this piece of mudstone, the broken spot is revealing a dark layer beneath it—it could be a fossil! Carefully breaking it open could reveal a leaf or other fossil.

Concretions are odd round rocks that often have a fossil inside. This one is still stuck in the limestone it formed within, and near it were lots of crinoid fossils.

If a rock looks to be full of fossils, it just might be! When many plants and animals died in one place, they sometimes turned into rock that is just full of fossils. This piece of limestone has little bits of trilobites and other ancient life.

Areas like this, with many layers that are safely accessed, are a treasure trove for fossil collectors. But never get too close to cliffs!

HOW DO YOU COLLECT FOSSILS?

When you begin to look for fossils (page 154 for information about where you can/cannot collect first), most of the first ones you will find will probably be loose or in small stones. That means that they won't be attached to a large rock formation and instead will be found on the ground. These fossils have been weathered free of their host rock, which means that weather like rain, ice, and wind has broken them from the rock they formed in. Loose fossils are most commonly found on beaches or along rivers; common examples include petrified wood and shells. To collect them, you simply pick them up! You should write down where you found them, too.

When you're a little better at finding fossils, you can start looking in formations of sedimentary rock for fossils still trapped in their host rock. When you find an outcropping of shale, for example, you can carefully use a tool or have an adult help you split apart the shale along its layers. Fossils can be found in between the layers of shale, and you can find them right where they've been hiding for millions of years! It's a lot more work to find fossils this way, but many times the fossils found this way are of better quality than the kind you find weathered loose.

This fossil trilobite fragment was hiding in between shale layers.

HOW SCIENTISTS COLLECT FOSSILS

A scientist who finds and studies fossils is called a **paleontologist**. Paleontologists collect fossils differently. Their goal is to safely collect as much of a fossil as possible. This way, they can learn as much as they can from it. When they find a big skeleton, like a dinosaur for example, they don't pick it up right away. Instead, they try to uncover as much as possible, using small tools like picks and soft brushes. When they've uncovered enough, then they coat the whole fossil in a material called plaster to protect it. After the plaster hardens, they carefully break the rock all around the fossil and take it back to their lab in one giant block. At the lab, they slowly chip away rock and reveal more and more of the fossil. Every part of the fossil is studied at the lab. This helps paleontologists learn as much about the animal as they can, including what it looked like, what it ate, and even how it moved! The rock around the fossil is very important, too, because it can tell us how old the fossil is and details about its environment, and all that information is then shared with other paleontologists.

Encasing a fossil in plaster

IDENTIFYING FOSSILS

Many times when you find a fossil, it won't look as nice as the ones in this book. That's because many millions of years have passed and in the process, many fossils were often broken or squished. This can make some fossils difficult to identify, especially if you only find a small piece. If so, you might need to contact a local school, museum, or rock shop for help figuring out what it is.

Even so, identifying fossils can be complicated and difficult, even for scientists. That's why it's very important to write down notes about what you find. Write down where you found it, mark down the GPS coordinates, and take pictures of the fossil in the rock, as this information, called context, can help experts identify your find. If it's a vertebrate fossil, leave it in the ground, and show your notes to an expert! That way, you're helping science!

Fossils as nice as this *Mesosaurus* are rare but very important to science.

Many small fossils of things like snails and shells are identified by comparing them with the ones that are alive today. Learning all about different kinds of snails, clams, oysters, corals, and plants can help you identify similar fossils. And by reading and learning about all kinds of fossils, animals, and plants, you'll be identifying fossils in no time!

ROCK SHOPS AND BUYING FOSSILS

Fossils are not always easy to find, and if you're not in the right place, you might not spot them. There is a good chance that you will see more fossils in a rock shop than you will in nature. Buying fossils is a good way to get neat specimens to study and learn from. Some fossils are more common in stores than others. When you're buying fossils, ask the store owner where they came from. That way you can learn more about them (and the rock they were found in) and confirm they were collected legally.

 Ammonites—The shells of these ancient squid-like creatures are very common and cheap in shops.

 **Orthoceras**—Many specimens of this shelled squid-like creature look like straight white shells in a dark rock. They are very common.

 **Amber**—Amber can be pricey, especially if there are bugs inside. Most specimens in shops have been polished.

 Shark teeth—Fossil shark teeth come in all sizes, shapes, and colors. They are usually common and cheap in shops, except for the huge teeth of the *megalodon*, which can be very expensive.

Crinoids and blastoids—These are very common fossils and most will be cheap. The biggest and most complete fossils, however, can be expensive.

Bivalves—Fossil clams and brachiopods are very common, and they are usually very cheap in stores.

Trilobites—Some trilobites are rarer and more expensive than others, but the most common and smallest ones are usually pretty cheap.

Corals—Fossil corals are very common, and even very large specimens can be inexpensive.

Ferns and plants—Small plant fossils like leaves and ferns are common and shouldn't cost very much. But very large specimens, or really cool ones with flowers or fruits, are rare and may be expensive.

Petrified wood—Most petrified wood is inexpensive, but some large or very colorful pieces can be very valuable.

REPLICAS

Not every fossil you'll see in stores is real. The *T. rex* teeth you'll probably see in stores are **replicas**. These are copies of real fossils made by covering a fossil in plaster.

This replica *T. rex* tooth looks just like a real one, but it is much cheaper to buy.

When the plaster hardened, it had the same shape as the real fossil. This mold is used to make copies that are then painted to look real. But replicas are a great way to learn about fossils you otherwise can't collect!

FAKE FOSSILS

Sometimes, sellers (especially those online) create fake fossils. They do so because it's difficult and expensive to get real ones or because the fossils aren't as easy to see as buyers expect. So when buying fossils (especially online), you have to look and choose carefully.

For example, some fossils are very pale and hard to see. Fossils of soft animals, like jellyfish or insects, are sometimes very faint and the same color as the rock they are found in. Sometimes the people who find fossils like these will use a special paint to color the fossil so that it is easier to see. And sometimes they will draw on details that were not even there! Shrimp fossils, for example, are often missing their little legs and antennae, but some fossil sellers draw them on so that they look better.

For a look at some of the most commonly faked fossils, see below.

When this fossil fish was found, it was hard to see, so it was painted darker. But see the fin on its back? The bones there are missing. The fin was painted on so the fossil looks complete.

Mosasaur teeth are very common. Sometimes the teeth are attached to a fake jaw bone and then put into a fake rock. This makes it look like a fossil mouth or jaw of a mosasaur, which are rarer and worth more money, but only the teeth are really real.

Copal looks a lot like amber, but it's not the same thing (page 133). Still, some shops try to sell it as amber.

COOL FOSSIL SITES AROUND THE U.S.

If you want to see some cool fossils no matter where you live in the United States, check out the list below. While you can't collect fossils at many of these places—check ahead before you go—you can still visit to see some amazing fossils and the rock formations they are found in! And these are just a sample—most states have many awesome places where fossils are found and fantastic museums to learn about them!

Alabama The banks of the river at Point A Dam, near Andalusia, are famous for revealing loose teeth of several species of shark and fish.

Alaska The Colville River, in northern Alaska, cuts through sedimentary rock formations and produces many fossils, including dinosaurs.

Arizona Petrified Forest National Park is a beautiful area with huge fossilized logs lying all over the colorful desert.

Arkansas The Buffalo National River system cuts through many rock formations that contain fossils. Collecting isn't allowed, but you can see shells, trace fossils, and more in the rock.

California The La Brea Tar Pits in Los Angeles are natural bubbling pools of oil where the bones of animals like saber-toothed tigers have been found.

Colorado Dinosaur National Monument, found in Colorado and Utah, has an amazing display of hundreds of dinosaur fossils still embedded in the face of a cliff.

Connecticut Dinosaur State Park in Rocky Hill protects hundreds of dinosaur footprints still in the rock, and it also has displays of fossils.

Delaware The Chesapeake and Delaware Canal, just south of Delaware City, cuts through some fossil-rich rock. You might find fossils on the shore, but also look in the sandy piles dumped on the shore near Reedy Point.

Florida The Venice Beach area is excellent for collecting fossil shark teeth that are found just lying in the sand.

Georgia Many of the coastal rivers and beaches around Savannah are famous for producing *megalodon* teeth.

Hawaii Though most of Hawaii is igneous and has no fossils, some fossil corals and shells have been found on the western shores of Oahu.

Idaho The Hagerman Fossil Beds National Monument is a beautiful area with beautiful layered rock formations where fantastic mammal fossils have been found, including horses.

Illinois The Mazon Creek formation, near Morris and Braidwood, is famous and important for its well-preserved fossils in concretions. Public collecting is allowed in the summer; check with the BLM or Illinois DNR for specific dates or changes in rules.

Indiana The Falls of the Ohio State Park in Clarksville has one of the largest exposures of Devonian reef fossils in the country. There you'll see corals, crinoids, and more still embedded in the rock.

Iowa Devonian Fossil Gorge, north of Iowa City, is loaded with ancient sea life fossils like corals and crinoids, still embedded in their host rock and easy to find and see.

Kansas Monument Rocks, south of Oakley, are the chalk remains of an ancient seafloor, and the area is full of fossil shells. You can't collect there, but you can see lots of ancient life.

The ground at Devonian Fossil Gorge, Iowa, is loaded with ancient sea life.

Kentucky Big Bone Lick State Park has indoor and outdoor fossil exhibits where you can see ancient life and learn about this important fossil site.

Louisiana The Cane River Site is one of the most famous in the state for fossils. It is a ridge along I-49 near Natchitoches with loads of sea life fossils, but be very careful near the highway.

Maine Fossils are scarce in Maine, but there are chances to find fossil sea life and seashell impressions in rocks all along the southern coasts.

Maryland Any beach along the Potomac River has the potential to turn up fossil shark teeth and other sea life, like snail shells.

Massachusetts Dinosaur tracks, or footprints, are Massachusetts' state fossil—you can see them near Holyoke along the Connecticut River at various famous outcroppings.

Michigan The Little Traverse Bay Area, near Petoskey and Charlevoix, is home to beaches where you can find Petoskey Stone, which is one of the most famous coral fossils in the U.S.

Petoskey Stone is Michigan's state fossil. It is a famous type of fossil coral.

Minnesota Northeastern Minnesota is home to the Gunflint Range, which is a formation of chert that contains stromatolites around 2 billion years old!

Mississippi The Dunn-Seiler Museum at Mississippi State University is home to an amazing collection of fossils, and staff can answer your fossil questions.

Missouri Missouri is known for its fantastic crinoid fossils. The area around Columbia produces many examples in local river beds and quarries.

Montana The Carter County Museum in Ekalaka has some of Montana's best fossils on display and can set you on the path to visit all the museums and sites along Montana's "Dinosaur Trail."

Nebraska Ashfall Fossil Beds State Historical Park lets you see dozens of fossil animals that died when a nearby volcano erupted—and they're all still in the rock where they were found.

Nevada You can see fossils of mammoths and other mammals right where they fell at Tule Springs Fossil Beds National Monument, near Las Vegas.

New Hampshire Fossils are pretty rare in New Hampshire, but you can see lots of them at the Woodman Institute Museum and the Children's Museum of New Hampshire, both in Dover.

New Jersey Lots of fossils can be found along the rivers near the coast—Big Brook is one river that produces shark teeth.

New Mexico The top of Sandia Crest, just outside of Albuquerque, is full of crinoids and other sea life fossils— on top of a mountain!

New York Much of western New York, especially the Buffalo area, is rich with sea life fossils. The Penn Dixie Fossil Park offers fossil-rich rock beds that you can hunt through.

North Carolina The Aurora Fossil Museum, in Aurora, has a large number of sea life fossils on display and offers fossil-rich piles of rock for kids to dig through for their own shark teeth!

North Dakota North Dakota is loaded with fossils. The North Dakota Geological Survey offers guided dig experiences to find your own fossils! Go to dmr.nd.gov for more information.

Ohio Fossil Park in Sylvania is great for kids because during the summer months the park provides fossil-rich shale that you can easily split apart and look in for fossils.

Oklahoma The area around Lake Texoma is famous for all different kinds of sea life fossils, and you can spot many still in their host rock. Collecting is only allowed with a permit, though.

Oregon All along Oregon's Pacific Coast, you can easily find fossil seashells embedded in sandstone, and petrified wood chunks.

The beach at Neskowin, Oregon, reveals the remains of a fossilized forest at low tide.

Pennsylvania
The banks of the Ohio River and roadcuts between Ambridge and Pittsburgh are loaded with fossil ferns, horsetails, and other ancient plants.

Rhode Island The beach just west of Portsmouth, at the end of Cory's Road, is well known for great fossil ferns and other plants in shale, and it is easy to get to.

South Carolina The Charleston area is rich with fossils of all kinds, especially shark teeth on the local beaches, such as Folly Beach. Local tour companies take families out on fossil-collecting tours.

South Dakota The Badlands are full of fossils of animals that thrived after the dinosaurs went extinct, including horses, camels, and birds.

Tennessee The Gray Fossil Site is an important location for fossil mammals and reptiles. The museum there has exhibits and live excavations to see fossils as they're found.

Texas You can walk along with the dinosaurs at Dinosaur Valley State Park, where multiple dinosaurs' footprints are preserved in rocks.

Utah The Utah Field House of Natural History State Park Museum has amazing fossils on display, with activities to help learn how to identify fossils, and even offers field trips to go find your own.

Vermont The Goodsell Ridge Fossil Preserve on Isle La Motte in Lake Champlain offers fossil tours that show off the ancient fossil reef and sea life fossils all over the island.

Virginia Fossil Beach, part of Westmoreland State Park, is known for its fossil shark teeth (including rare *megalodon* teeth!) in the sand and just offshore.

Washington You can see a "forest" of petrified ginkgo trees at Ginkgo Petrified Forest State Park.

West Virginia Quarries in the Lost River area, along the road west of Wardensville, are known for their wealth of trilobites, often collected with little extra effort.

Wisconsin Wisconsin is known for its trilobite and other sea life fossils, particularly along rivers and at outcroppings in the southern portion of the state, around Milwaukee.

Wyoming Wyoming is incredibly rich with fossils; the Fossil Butte National Monument has an incredible number of specimens on display and nature hikes to see where they are found.

Fossil Butte in Wyoming is a very important fossil site in the United States.

GLOSSARY

algae Simple aquatic plant-like organisms that don't have flowers or stems; algae include seaweed and many forms often known as "pond scum"

amphibian Cold-blooded vertebrates, such as frogs, that usually live in or near water, with young that have gills and adults that have lungs

arachnid Small arthropods that have a segmented body and eight legs

arthropod A group of cold-blooded invertebrate animals that have hard, armored bodies divided into segments, and jointed legs; arachnids, insects, and crustaceans are all arthropods

bacteria Microscopic (too small to see) organisms that are neither a plant nor an animal; they are the earliest forms of life on earth

bed A layer of sediment that becomes a layer in sedimentary rock when it hardens

bird Warm-blooded vertebrate animals with wings, feathers, scaly legs and feet, beaks, and that lay eggs; they are directly related to dinosaurs and can be considered a type of dinosaur

cells The tiny components that make up all living things, plant or animal; each cell is a compartment that contains the material a plant or animal needs to live, grow, make energy, and repair itself

cephalopod Invertebrate animals that have large heads and tentacles, such as squid or octopus; ammonites were cephalopods, for example

crustacean A group of arthropod animals that have hard, segmented bodies, live mostly in water, and lay eggs; crabs, barnacles, and shrimp are crustaceans

decay The process of a plant or animal rotting away

diatoms Microscopic algae that have hard shells made of silica (a material like quartz)

dinosaur Complex vertebrate animals that first appeared in the Triassic period; they evolved from reptiles but were likely warm-blooded; they included meat-eaters and plant-eaters, and some walked on two legs and others four; some were solitary and others lived in herds; they laid eggs, had scaly skin, and many had feathers; birds evolved from dinosaurs

dissolve When a material disappears and becomes incorporated into water

extinct When a plant or animal dies out; when there are none left

fossil The remains of a plant or animal that have turned into minerals

fossilize When the remains of a plant or animal are turned into minerals after being buried and exposed to mineral-rich water or sediment

geological period The way scientists organize the history of the Earth; periods are defined by major changes on earth, such as extinctions

igneous Rocks that formed when molten rock cooled and hardened

insect Small arthropods that usually have a hard outer body, six legs, and usually have wings

invertebrate Animals that don't have a spine, or backbone

mammal Warm-blooded vertebrate animals that have fur or hair and produce milk for their young

metamorphic Rocks that formed when older rocks were heated and/or pressed within the earth

microscopic Something too small to see with just your eye

mineral A substance that forms when a pure chemical hardens; minerals form as crystals inside rocks.

modern Something from recent, not ancient, times

mollusk Invertebrate animals with soft unsegmented bodies; they usually have a hard outer shell and live in water

myriapod Small arthropods that have long bodies and many legs; millipedes and centipedes are examples

outcropping An exposure of rock; where rock layers can be seen without plants or other things covering them up

paleontologist A scientist who studies fossil life

plankton A mixture of mostly microscopic animals and organisms that float in the oceans; plankton can also include tiny plants and algae

predator An animal that hunts and eats other animals

preserve When the original state of an object or material is maintained; for example, fossilization can preserve, or keep, the tiny veins in a leaf

prey An animal that is hunted and eaten by other animals

reptile Cold-blooded vertebrates that have dry scaly skin, lungs, and don't need to live in water; lizards and snakes are examples of reptiles

rock A hard mixture of minerals; the earth is made up of rocks

sediment Tiny particles of various materials, usually rocks (in the form of sand or mud), plant matter, or animals (such as diatom skeletons) that are easily moved by wind and water; sediment settles into beds that may eventually harden to become sedimentary rock

sedimentary Rocks that formed when sediment hardened

settle When sediment sinks to the bottom of a body of water

scientific name The special name that scientists use to refer to an individual plant, animal, or life-form; each type of life gets a genus name (say it "gee-nus") and a species name (say it "spee-sheez"); the genus names are like a last name and are capitalized and in italic; species names are in lowercase, and also italicized, and sort of like a first name

species A single group of animals that have similar features and can produce babies together

spine A backbone; animals with a spine are vertebrates

vertebrate Animals that have a spine, or backbone

RECOMMENDED READING FOR KIDS

Lynch, Dan R. *Rock Collecting for Kids: An Introduction to Geology*. Cambridge: Adventure Publications, 2018.

Tomecek, Steve. *National Geographic Kids: Everything Rocks and Minerals*. National Geographic, 2011.

Romaine, Garret. *Geology Lab for Kids*. Minneapolis: Quarto Publishing, 2017.

RECOMMENDED READING FOR OLDER READERS

Robinson, George W. *Minerals*. New York: Simon & Schuster, 1994.

Pough, Frederick H. *A Field Guide to Rocks and Minerals*. Boston: Houghton Mifflin, 1988.

Walker, Cyril, and Ward, David. *Smithsonian Handbooks: Fossils*. New York: DK Publishing, 2002.

Lindsay, William. *Prehistoric Life*. New York: DK Publishing, 1994.

Coenraads, Robert R. *Rocks & Fossils: A Visual Guide*. Sydney: Firefly Books, 2005.

Lynch, Dan R. *Petoskey Stone: Finding, Identifying, and Collecting Michigan's Most Storied Fossil*. Cambridge: Adventure Publications, 2019.

ABOUT THE AUTHOR

Dan R. Lynch grew up in a rock shop, learning how to identify rocks, minerals, and fossils from a very young age. Since then, he's written over 20 books about rock and mineral identification, with a special focus on agates from his home region of northern Minnesota and Lake Superior. He has always loved the natural world, especially all of its wonderful little details that most people don't pay any attention to and the amazing history behind them. With his children's books, he hopes to spark young readers' curiosities in the rocks beneath their feet and in all of the incredible ancient species that came before us. Dan currently lives in Madison, Wisconsin, with his wife, Julie, and their cat, Daisy.

The Flickr images below are licensed under the Public Domain Dedication (CC0 1.0) license, which is available here: https://creativecommons.org/publicdomain/
Gary Todd: 59 (top).

Images used under license from Shutterstock.com:
Aaron Amat: 40 (right); **Aerial-motion:** 77 (bottom); **Albert Russ:** 20 (right); **Aleksandr Pobedimskiy:** 36 (bottom), 38 (top left gray), 148 (right); **AlessandroZocc:** 29 (bottom); **Andrei Nekrassov:** 68 (bottom); **Ansis Klucis:** 107 (bottom left), 175 (bottom middle); **Arndale:** 140 (bottom); **Atypeek Dsgn:** 69 (top right); **AuntSpray:** 98 (bottom); **B Brown:** 112-113; **Barbol:** 26 (middle); **Beliphotos:** 46 (left); **Bildagentur Zoonar GmbH:** 80 (top left); **Breck P. Kent:** 11 (middle right), 126 (top right), 149 (bottom), 173 (Ferns and plants); **Buquet Christophe:** 99 (middle); **Butterfly Hunter:** 118; **CatbirdHill:** 174; **Choksawatdikorn:** 144 (left); **Chris Hoff:** 152; **COULANGES:** 89 (bottom right); **Cristina Romero Palma:** 107 (crane fly); **Dafinchi:** 173 (Petrified wood); **DariaRen:** 114 (right); **David Herraez Calzada:** 58 (top); **David Tran Photo:** 146 (top left); **Dennis Sabo:** 101 (bottom); **Digital Photo:** 26 (left); **Dinoton:** 13 (bottom left); **Domnitsky:** 16-17 (sand); **Dotted Yeti:** 55 (bottom left), 62 (top), 111 (bottom left); **Dr. Norbert Lange:** 38 (bottom right), 138; **EcoPrint:** 8 (bottom left); **Edelwipix:** 149 (top); **Emma Jones:** 98 (middle); **Erlantz P.R:** 57 (inset); **Ermess:** 22 (left); **gan chaonan:** 83 (bottom right); **Gartland:** 18 (top), 168; **Ging o_o:** 141 (top); **gnanistock:** 64 (top left); **gorosan:** 59 (bottom); **gracious_tiger:** 132 (top left); **Gregory Pelt:** 41 (bottom inset); **Gsaielli:** 71 (bottom right); **Guido Bainat:** 151 (bottom right); **gunungkawi:** 159 (right); **Herschel Hoffmeyer:** 9 (top), 53 (top), 53 (bottom), 55 (middle), 56 (bottom left), 58 (bottom); **HotFlash:** 102; **Iakov Kalinin:** 119 (palms); **icedmocha:** 52 (bottom); **Ihor Bondarenko:** 144 (right); **Iryna Terekh:** 164 (bottom); **Ivan Smuk:** 175 (middle); **Jacob Boomsma:** 178; **Jef Wodniack:** 136; **Jim and Lynne Weber:** 27 (top right), 60 (bottom right); **Jung Hsuan:** 19 (middle left); **kevin brine:** 15 (top); **Kichigin:** 104 (top left); **kojihirano:** 18-19 (background); **Kotomiti Okuma:** 40 (left); **Krikkiat:** 69 (top left); **KrimKate:** 140 (top left); **lcrms:** 99 (bottom); **Lesleyanne Ryan:** 137; **Linnas:** 10 (bottom); **Lotus_studio:** 86 (middle right); **LukaKikina:** 41 (main); **m.afiqsyahmi:** 146 (bottom); **Maciej Bledowski:** 52 (top); **MarcelClemens:** 67 (bottom right), 104 (middle left); **Maria Arts:** 133; **Marius Rudzianskas:** 134 (top); **mark higgins:** 22 (right), 50, 70, 141 (bottom); **Martin Voeller:** 67 (middle); **meyblume:** 101 (top left); **Michael Rosskothen:** 13 (top); **Michael Warwick:** 181; **MikhailSh:** 49 (#2); **Miroslav Halama:** 64 (top right); **MPSilva:** 15 (bottom); **Nadia Yong:** 124; **ND700:** 117; **Netta Arobas:** 46 (right); **Neuroplastic Creative:** 159 (left); **Noiel:** 55 (bottom right); **nostalgi1@mail.ru:** 73; **olpo:** 21 (bottom); **Pakhnyushchy:** 82 (main); **paleontologist natural:** 54, 157, 170; **Paulo Afonso:** 101 (top right); **Puwadol Jaturawutthichai:** 6-7, 55 (top left), 111 (top right); **Rattiya Thongdumhyu:** 16 (inset); **Rich Koele:** 111 (bottom right); **Sascha Burkard:** 34 (bottom right); **Savvapanf Photo:** 126 (bottom left); **Scisetti Alfio:** 116 (middle); **Sebastian Kaulitzki:** 95 (top left); **Sergei Mironenko:** 49 (#4); **Servickuz:** 114 (left); **Shawn Hempel:** 126 (top left); **SHTRAUS DMYTRO:** 148 (left); **Simon Shin kwangsig:** 89 (middle left); **Skye Studio LK:** 18 (middle); **solarseven:** 41 (top inset), 61 (top); **Sombra:** 13 (middle); **Steven Russell Smith Ohio:** 71 (bottom left); **Subbotina Anna:** 19 (top left); **Susilull:** 158; **Sven Hoppe:** 129 (top left); **Svineyard:** 38 (top left, gold); **Tom Grundy:** 116 (bottom right); **TR_Studio:** 175 (bottom left); **Tristan Brynildsen:** 182; **Valzan:** 147; **Vangert:** 151 (top right); **Warpaint:** 13 (bottom right), 53 (middle), 69 (middle); **Wlad74:** 57 (bottom); **Wolfilser:** 12 (left); **www.sandatlas.org:** 37 (middle left, dark); **Zack Frank:** 132 (bottom); **Zaferkizilkaya:** 86 (bottom middle); **Zerbor:** 125; **zimowa:** 27 (top left).